Beyond Algorithms

Beyond Algorithms: Reframing AI as Intellectual Capital for Human Flourishing offers a clear, timely framework for viewing and analyzing AI as intellectual capital rather than as autonomous intelligence. AI is presented as a tool that helps organize, expand, and apply knowledge to support human decision-making, improve institutional effectiveness, and promote social progress. By situating AI as capital within the broader view of capital development, the book offers a balanced perspective that avoids narratives that depict technology as either a savior or a threat.

Building on theories of capital, institutional economics, education research, and current AI research, the book introduces a six-capital framework: human, intellectual, structural, physical, financial, and ethical capital. This framework clarifies how AI transforms both profit-oriented and mission-driven organizations, where concepts such as productivity, accountability, and legitimacy are understood differently. The book explains why initial AI implementations often led to misalignment, risks, and vulnerabilities, and emphasizes that ethical capital, governance, and boundary-setting are vital for aligning AI with institutional goals. It offers practical guidance on aligning capital, AI governance, measurement, and decision-making. Additionally, *Beyond Algorithms* provides tools for assessing AI investments and organizational readiness in market and public-interest settings.

This book is intended for scholars, social scientists, advanced students, policymakers, technology practitioners, and business, education, government, and civil society leaders who seek a rigorous, accessible approach to AI that prioritizes human development, institutional integrity, and long-term value creation over short-term optimization.

Roderic Hewlett is an economist and former professor with international experience in business, finance, and education. His work examines how capital theory, technology, economics, ethics, and knowledge underpin human and social progress, and how AI influences institutions, governance, and human well-being.

Beyond Algorithms
Reframing AI as Intellectual Capital for Human Flourishing

Roderic Hewlett

CRC Press

Taylor & Francis Group

Boca Raton London New York

CRC Press is an imprint of the
Taylor & Francis Group, an **informa** business

A CHAPMAN & HALL BOOK

Designed cover image: Shutterstock

First edition published 2027
by CRC Press
2385 NW Executive Center Drive, Suite 320, Boca Raton FL 33431

and by CRC Press
4 Park Square, Milton Park, Abingdon, Oxon, OX14 4RN

CRC Press is an imprint of Taylor & Francis Group, LLC

Library of Congress Cataloging-in-Publication Data
Names: Hewlett, Roderic, 1958- author
Title: Beyond algorithms : reframing AI as intellectual capital for human
flourishing / Roderic Hewlett.
Description: First edition. | Boca Raton, FL : CRC Press, 2027. | Includes
bibliographical references and index.
Identifiers: LCCN 2026012319 (print) | LCCN 2026012320 (ebook) | ISBN
9781041248873 hbk | ISBN 9781041248866 pbk | ISBN 9781003744061 ebk
Subjects: LCSH: Capital | Artificial intelligence--Social aspects |
Artificial intelligence--Economic aspects
Classification: LCC HB501 .H474 2027 (print) | LCC HB501 (ebook)
LC record available at https://lccn.loc.gov/2026012319
LC ebook record available at https://lccn.loc.gov/2026012320

ISBN: 978-1-041-24887-3 (hbk)
ISBN: 978-1-041-24886-6 (pbk)
ISBN: 978-1-003-74406-1 (ebk)

DOI: 10.1201/9781003744061

Typeset in Minion
by SPi Technologies India Pvt Ltd (Straive)

Contents

Illustrations

CHAPTER 1

Artificial Intelligence at the Crossroads of Hype and Hope

EXTENDING HUMAN ABILITY

Artificial intelligence (AI) is often described as a societal inflection point, a sudden leap into an unfamiliar future. It certainly adds remarkable new capabilities to the tools that support human action. In truth, AI belongs to a much longer story. It continues the centuries-old project of building technologies that extend human thought, organize knowledge, and amplify judgment. From writing systems and libraries to calculators and computers, technology has always served as intellectual support for human beings. AI does not replace what makes us uniquely human. It sharpens our effectiveness, accelerates our work, and expands our creative reach. Like earlier breakthroughs, AI will reshape how we learn, create, communicate, govern, and solve problems. Yet, it remains part of the same narrative: human ingenuity building tools that leverage human ability, for better or worse, depending on how wisely the tools are used.

Tasks that once demanded significant effort, repetition, and time can now be completed with fewer steps, less strain, and greater precision. AI increases the return on human effort. More specifically, it enhances human capital, the accumulated store of knowledge, skills, judgment, experience, and capabilities unique to each person. Fears that AI will render originality unnecessary are misplaced. When used wisely, AI reduces waste, accelerates drafting and revision, and opens pathways to new creative insights. The spark remains human. AI broadens the range and speed of expression. Yet AI has limits. It creates new dependencies, requires careful oversight, and adds gravity to human judgment. Used casually, it can mislead, distort, and create false impressions. Like many developments in the history of capital, AI brings both promise and risk.

Every generation imagines its tools to be uniquely revolutionary. AI is no exception. The hopes, anxieties, and bold predictions surrounding it echo earlier moments in technological history. Mechanization, electrification, and computing each arrived with waves of enthusiasm, disappointment, correction, and eventual maturity. AI follows the same trajectory. It comes with great expectations, encounters limits, undergoes refinement, and, when guided well, becomes an integrated contributor to human capability.

Human history is marked by invention, expansion, misapplication, and eventual wisdom. Understanding AI within this pattern requires understanding capital itself. Human capital describes people's capacity, or skills and abilities, to learn, create, judge, and decide. Capital more broadly refers to the resources and supporting structures that expand what humans can accomplish. Tools, infrastructure, institutions, knowledge systems, and technologies are expressions of capital that extend human reach. AI stands within this tradition as a powerful form of leverage. Each incremental increase in capital, however, requires corresponding increases in education, culture, governance, and ethical formation so that technology serves human purposes rather than distorting them. Hype obscures this reality. Real progress depends on disciplined human development.

When capital is understood correctly, the trajectory of technology becomes clearer. Capital advances economic and social life not by replacing humanity but by strengthening the effectiveness of human uniqueness. When tools are wisely governed and aligned with human needs, they amplify potential. Although still emerging, AI already demonstrates this amplifying effect.

The narrative of capital, especially regarding AI, must also account for its influence on culture, work, community, leisure, and education. AI extends human capacity to transform information into meaningful action. It calls for renewed attention to truthfulness, data integrity, interpretation, and refined probability. When deployed without proper insight, AI may dampen human flourishing, deepen confusion, and cause harm. As an evolving form of capital, AI remains unfinished. Its value depends on the strength of human beings and institutions, and on the ethical commitments that guide them.

UNIQUE NATURE OF HUMANS

Human existence occupies a singular position in the known world, defined by sentience, relational capacity, and an orientation toward intentional development. Unlike other creatures whose behavior remains largely instinctual or environmentally constrained, human beings can reflect, imagine, initiate, and reshape reality. Hannah Arendt describes this as natality, the capacity to begin, to introduce something genuinely new into the world through judgment and creativity (Arendt 1998, 9). Through this distinctive endowment, human communities move beyond survival into cultures shaped by meaning, aspiration, and purposeful advancement.

Human life unfolds as a continual process of growth, creativity, invention, care, support, and communal development. Each person follows a unique path that shapes perception, attention, thought, judgment, and action. Decisions and consequences are not merely programmed outputs or statistical predictions. They are human responses rooted in conscience, memory, hope, and responsibility. Societies develop knowledge systems, nurture scientific and artistic achievement, protect the vulnerable, and sustain practices that serve the common good. Technology, including AI, may extend human capability, yet it does not share the existential depth of embodied consciousness, moral discernment, emotional reciprocity, or intergenerational responsibility. Scholars such as Charles Taylor (1992) and Alasdair MacIntyre (1981) describe human identity as emerging through narrative, virtue, relationships, and purpose, realms beyond the reach of algorithmic approximation. Through these qualities, human beings remain the creators and governors of intellectual capital rather than its servants.

Human uniqueness is most evident in capacities for reason, imagination, discernment, and moral evaluation. These capacities are not exercised in isolation. They gain traction through the support societies construct around them, support that takes the form of capital. In contemporary scholarship, capital refers not only to money, markets, or financial assets (Bourdieu 2021). It encompasses the tangible and intangible resources that extend human capability, enhance the quality of action, and shape the outcomes of decisions. Each form of capital operates as a scaffold that strengthens human ability to innovate, discover, repair, teach, govern, and care.

Viewed in this light, the development of capital becomes one of the central stories of human progress. Different forms of capital, including human, intellectual, structural, physical, financial, and ethical capital, work together to expand what people and communities can accomplish. Within this framework, AI appears not as a rival to the human person but as a developing expression of intellectual capital. The terminology surrounding AI varies, describing it as a method, an intangible asset, or data that feed into the creation of human knowledge (Varian 2018). While these terms may be imprecise, they point to AI as an intellectual supplement to human agency. It channels, organizes, and amplifies knowledge. It supports rather than supplants human agency, creativity, and judgment.

This understanding prepares the ground for the next step. To see clearly how AI participates in human advancement, the foundations that sustain human progress must be understood. Capital in its many forms provides that foundation and shapes how societies grow, innovate, and flourish across generations.

CAPITAL AS THE FOUNDATION OF HUMAN PROGRESS

At the heart of every enduring economic and social change lies capital. The term is often reduced to money, financial assets, or technical market instruments. A broader view reveals that capital encompasses any resource, tangible or intangible, that drives change, increases productivity, fosters innovation, enhances problem-solving, and generates returns through added value (Stewart 1997; Roos et al. 1997; Davenport and Prusak 2000). In this broader sense, capital serves both as fuel for human progress and as one of its clearest indicators (Bourdieu 2021).

From the vantage point of human uniqueness, capital can be understood as a set of supportive structures that help human abilities take root and mature. Education systems, knowledge repositories, institutions, tools, financial resources, and moral cultures do not replace human agency. They create environments in which judgment, creativity, and responsibility flourish. Capital enables insight to become practice and local effort to extend outward into broader social benefit. In this sense, capital forms the architecture through which human potential becomes productive reality.

A concise introduction to six interconnected forms of capital provides a framework for understanding how societies absorb, adapt to, and redirect technological change. This framework is essential in the context of AI, which interacts with each form by amplifying human capabilities, accelerating knowledge flows, reshaping organizational structures, and altering the purpose and value of work. Each form of capital contributes in distinct but interdependent ways to how individuals, communities, and organizations innovate, create, govern, and grow. The following sections introduce these six forms of capital and describe how they support human flourishing across social, economic, and personal life.

Within this capital framework, AI is not a rival to the human person but a developing expression of intellectual capital. It channels, organizes, and amplifies knowledge. It supports rather than supplants human agency, creativity, and judgment.

Human Capital

Human capital refers to a distinctive set of acquired capacities rather than to the essence of what it means to be human. Human uniqueness arises from deeper intellectual, moral, and creative dimensions. Human capital encompasses the cultivated skills, knowledge, abilities, refined talents, behaviors, and dispositions that enable effective action in the world (Becker 1994; Schultz 1961). It includes formal education, technical proficiency, health and well-being, emotional intelligence, maturity, physical capability, and accumulated life experience (Mincer 1974).

Human capital is both situational and context dependent. A master accountant may have little aptitude for plumbing, just as a skilled surgeon may lack architectural ability. Some higher-order abilities, such as problem-solving, communication, contextual judgment, and pattern recognition, can transfer across settings. Even so, most competencies remain shaped by environments, vocations, expectations, and deliberate training. These differences reveal the extent to which human capital depends on the settings that cultivate or constrain growth (Mincer 1974; Davenport 1999).

The full promise of human capital emerges only when other forms of capital support it. When linked with intellectual, structural, physical, financial, and ethical capital, human capital becomes a powerful pool of abilities that supports human agency in innovation, coordination, and value creation. These complementary forms of capital provide the channels, scaffolds, and extensions through which cultivated abilities achieve their full effect.

AI as a Complement and Amplifier of Human Capital

AI reshapes human capital not by replacing individuals but by altering which skills matter most for effective action. AI is not human capital. It functions as supporting intellectual capital, comprising explicit knowledge, structured models, algorithms, computing capabilities, and recorded reasoning that can be stored, shared, scaled, and reused (Brynjolfsson and Mitchell 2017; Davenport and Ronanki 2018). In this capacity, AI provides analytical support, accessible and explicit knowledge, and adaptive tools that extend and refine human capabilities.

Because AI primarily operates on explicit knowledge and pattern recognition, it underscores the importance of human capacities that remain tacit, embodied, and unique. Creativity, ethical judgment, situational awareness, relational understanding, and the ability to frame problems wisely become increasingly valuable as routine cognitive tasks migrate to digital systems. Interpretation, meaning-making, judgment, choice, consequence management, and responsibility remain human endeavors.

As AI becomes enmeshed in physical, structural, and financial systems, the productivity of human capital increasingly depends on the ability to interpret, supervise, critique, and guide AI-enabled processes. Human beings move from solitary problem solvers to stewards of augmented systems. Human discernment, creativity, judgment, action, and responsibility determine whether AI contributes to flourishing or accelerates fragmentation. In this relationship, AI is explicit intellectual capital. It remains a tool that organizes and applies knowledge, while human judgment directs its purpose and limits.

SIDEBAR 1.1 FOUNDATIONS OF HUMAN CAPITAL AND AI RELEVANCE

Human capital is an investment in people. Over decades of scholarship, several enduring insights about investment have emerged.

- Human capital grows through intentional, focused investments. Theodore W. Schultz showed that education, training, and health are purposeful investments that enhance both personal capability and social productivity.
- Human capital is an asset with variable returns. Gary Becker demonstrated that knowledge, experience, and skill generate value in different ways, depending on incentives, opportunities, and choices.
- Human capital develops in context. Jacob Mincer emphasized that experience, specialization, and accumulated time in a role shape capability, performance, and long-term outcomes.

- Human–machine collaboration strengthens work. Thomas Davenport and Rajeev Ronanki showed that AI improves performance when it supports judgment, structures information, and aids decision-making rather than replacing human responsibility.

AI relevance. AI does not diminish the need for human capital. It heightens it. As routine work automates, the most valuable abilities become judgment, creativity, interpretation, ethical reasoning, and the capacity to supervise and integrate AI wisely.

Synthesis. Human capital provides direction, meaning, and moral grounding. AI extends reach, speed, and analytical capacity. Progress depends on developing people first and then building systems that responsibly support them.

Intellectual Capital

Intellectual capital is grounded in organized explicit knowledge, cultivated expertise, and shared understanding. It is augmented and tailored for application by tacit human insight, the ways of knowing that silently guide perception, judgment, and practice even when they cannot be fully articulated (Polanyi 2019; Felin and Holweg 2024). Intellectual capital encompasses the explicit elements of *know-what, know-how,* and *know-why* that shape professional intelligence across domains such as innovation, design, diagnosis, problem-solving, repair, and teamwork. These dimensions clarify how knowledge supports performance in complex environments (Quinn, Anderson, and Finkelstein 1996).

Intellectual capital is never confined to an individual mind. It unfolds through books, journals, archives, patents, data repositories, and digital libraries. It lives in professional traditions, scientific fields, apprenticeships, mentorship relationships, and communities of practice. It is stored not only as information but also as accumulated understanding, constantly tested, challenged, refined, and renewed across generations (Stewart 1997).

As scholars of intellectual capital argue, knowledge is most powerful when supported by structures that enable its sharing, preservation, refinement, and reuse. Human insight expands when intellectual capital is embedded in systems, routines, standards, technologies, and networks that ensure knowledge remains accessible even as people and roles change (Roos et al. 1997). In this way, intellectual capital interacts with structural capital to create stability, repeatability, and coordinated action.

Intellectual capital's importance becomes most evident when it is meaningfully linked to human capital. When skilled individuals can access the proper knowledge at the right time, their judgment sharpens, their creativity becomes more fully grounded, and their decision-making becomes more reliable. Intellectual capital provides frameworks that clarify complex problems, procedural knowledge that strengthens craftsmanship, and accumulated experience that reduces preventable errors. Knowledge becomes valuable when it is contextual, experience based, and action oriented (Davenport and Prusak 2000).

The crucial transformation occurs when raw data and scattered information are organized into actionable guidance. Intellectual capital does not merely store facts. It provides context that helps interpret, integrate, and direct those facts toward wise choices. When external knowledge, or intellectual capital, is internalized through human action, reflected upon, refined, and applied, it becomes a unique human resource for discovery, growth, productivity, and development.

Within this framework, AI clearly belongs to the family of intellectual capital rather than standing apart from it. AI operates as explicit, coded, reusable knowledge, embodied in models, rules, and computational systems that organize information at scale (Brynjolfsson and Mitchell 2017). It can retrieve, compare, simulate, and suggest. Yet, it lacks moral purpose, conscience, or the wisdom required to govern its own use beyond its design and training protocol. Its value depends entirely on the people and organizations that shape, direct, supervise, and apply it.

Properly cultivated, intellectual capital becomes a bridge linking discovery with practice, creativity with discipline, and human imagination with structured knowledge. When combined with human capital, structural supports, and ethical guidance, intellectual capital strengthens all other forms of capital. It is one of the most critical levers by which societies learn, innovate, and flourish.

SIDEBAR 1.2   INTELLECTUAL CAPITAL AND AI, KNOWLEDGE THAT EXTENDS

What is intellectual capital. Intellectual capital is society's accumulated store of knowledge: the ideas, concepts, methods, and insights that enable people and organizations to understand, create, and solve problems. It grows through discovery, documentation, reflection, experimentation, and shared learning (Stewart 1997; Roos et al. 1997).

Why it matters

- It helps people frame problems clearly.
- It supports skilled craftsmanship and technical excellence.
- It reduces avoidable errors by drawing on prior experience.
- It accelerates innovation by building on what has already been learned.

(Quinn, Anderson, and Finkelstein 1996)

Where AI fits. AI operates as *explicit intellectual capital*: structured, recorded, and reusable knowledge that can be stored, shared, and applied at scale (Brynjolfsson and Mitchell 2017). AI can:

- expand access to information
- reveal patterns too complex to see alone
- support decision-making and analysis
- preserve and transmit accumulated understanding

What AI cannot do. AI does not generate conscience, wisdom, purpose, or virtue. It cannot replace tacit human judgment, moral reasoning, creativity, or relational discernment (Polanyi 2019). Without guidance, it risks amplifying confusion rather than insight.

Synthesis. When AI is governed wisely, it strengthens intellectual capital by making knowledge more accessible, organized, and usable. Human beings remain responsible for directing how that knowledge is applied, ensuring that technology serves human flourishing rather than subordinating people to systems.

Structural Capital

Structural capital is the framework that integrates knowledge, behavior, and authority. It is the governance architecture through which societies and organizations preserve what they know, coordinate their actions, and ensure continuity over time. Structural capital includes constitutions and laws, charters and bylaws, policies and procedures, routines and practices, reporting systems, incentives, communication channels, and the cultural norms that guide conduct.

Structural capital complements intellectual capital by providing a governance structure for knowledge. As Thomas Stewart (1997) observes, structural capital encompasses entrenched knowledge and the processes and systems that enable activity to continue reliably even as people change roles or depart. Similarly, structural capital can be described as the architecture that enables knowledge to expand, becoming repeatable, coordinated, and collectively accessible (Roos et al. 1997). When used well, AI is aligned, channeled, and governed through social and organizational structures, or structural capital.

Structural capital not only shapes what organizations do but also aligns human activity through its governing role. Charles Taylor (1992) notes that human identity is formed within moral frameworks, social practices, and shared narratives that give meaning to action. Alasdair MacIntyre (1981) likewise argues that practices, traditions, and institutions cultivate virtues or erode them, depending on how they are organized and governed. Structural capital is further shaped by an ethical dimension: systems either encourage integrity, responsibility, and stewardship or move people toward compliance, self-interest, and short-term calculation.

A crucial distinction clarifies how structural capital governs social and economic life. It is institutional by nature. Institutions are the documented fabric of structural capital, comprising overarching rules such as constitutions, laws, legal orders, and governance codes that define legitimate and predictable action. They also encompass the unwritten but binding threads of culture, norms, standards, and beliefs. Organizations operate within those institutional boundaries. Structural capital includes both the institutional horizons that define what is right and possible and the organizational mechanisms that translate rules into daily practice. Structural capital is a shaping component of human and intellectual capital.

When well designed, structural capital creates appropriate channels for creativity, productivity, and innovation by reducing social ambiguity, clarifying authority, and aligning behavior through a shared purpose. It channels human, intellectual, physical, and financial capital into coordinated action. Structural capital can foster trust, transparency, learning, and adaptation. When poorly designed, e.g., overly rigid, lacking transparency, overly complex, outdated, or unjust, it fragments systems, slows responses, undermines trust, and limits what even competent people and wise ideas can accomplish.

Structural capital is not mere administration. It is the pathway through which purpose becomes policy, policy becomes practice, and practice shapes culture. It either enables the flourishing of other forms of capital or quietly constrains their potential.

SIDEBAR 1.3   STRUCTURAL CAPITAL, GOVERNANCE THAT MAKES KNOWLEDGE WORK

What structural capital includes

- constitutions, charters, bylaws, and legal frameworks
- policies, procedures, standards, and protocols
- organizational charts and decision pathways
- documentation, records, and communication systems
- norms, customs, expectations, incentives, and culture

Why it matters

- preserves knowledge when roles change
- clarifies authority and responsibility
- reduces confusion, duplication, and risk
- supports accountability and trust
- makes coordinated action possible.

The human dimension. Institutions and systems shape character. They form habits, expectations, and moral imagination, for better or for worse (Taylor 1992; MacIntyre 1981).

AI connection. AI depends on strong governance. Without oversight, transparency, review, and ethical direction, AI heightens risk. With clear structural capital, AI strengthens institutions rather than destabilizing them.

Guiding principle. Good structure is not bureaucracy. It is governance ordered toward people, wisdom, knowledge, and the common good.

Physical Capital

Physical capital is the most visible form of enabling capital: the tangible infrastructure, tools, spaces, and material resources that enable people, organizations, and societies to build, create, heal, and flourish. It includes laboratories, workshops, factories, classrooms, clinics, transportation systems, communication networks, and the physical tools of daily life. At a more fundamental level, physical capital also encompasses the natural world, including land, water, air, minerals, forests, and ecosystems that support every human activity.

Traditional accounting distinguishes between depreciable capital assets and short-lived expenses. These distinctions do not fully capture how physical capital functions. Even temporary, consumable, or rapidly outdated assets may play decisive roles in experimentation, learning, and innovation. These essential physical items are expensed and do not appear on financial balance sheets. Likewise, the natural world is not merely a stock of resources to be extracted. It is the sustaining environment that makes life and creativity possible; how it is used or misused shapes the future capacity of every other form of capital. The natural world does not appear on an organization's balance sheet, yet it materially affects all aspects of its operations. Physical capital comprises the physical aspects of the world, including natural and manufactured resources that sustain daily life.

Economic and technological research supports this broader understanding. Foundational growth models treat physical capital as a central productive input that increases output and creates opportunities for technological progress (Solow 1956; Jorgenson 1963). Innovation studies show that tools, prototypes, testing environments, pilot plants, and early stage hardware are essential to discovery because they invite trial, failure, revision, and refinement (Rosenberg 1983; Teece 1986; Von Hippel 2006). Physical capital extends beyond standard accounting treatments.

The often unseen value of physical capital lies in its capacity to expand understanding. Prototypes expose limits. Laboratories reveal weaknesses. Work environments show where ideas break and how they can be strengthened. Nature reveals profound truths and demonstrates the essence of sustainable systems. Research suggests that the most significant returns often go to those who learn from earlier investments and inventions and then adapt or extend them (Teece 1986; Von Hippel 2006). Many of these investments and inventions are physical. These observable attributes of physical presence can obscure the human ingenuity, intellectual contributions, and the structural framework that made these breakthroughs and investments possible. Capital is interconnected.

The integrated nature of capital becomes especially clear in the field of AI. AI is often described as virtual, yet it is profoundly physical. Chips, compute clusters, robotics platforms, sensors, cooling systems, cyberphysical components, and data centers require minerals, manufacturing capacity, land, water, and electricity. These assets age quickly and require continual reinvestment (Brynjolfsson, Rock, and Syverson 2017; Agrawal, Gans, and Goldfarb 2018). Benefits accrue gradually through upgrades, recalibrations, and new applications. As Hal Varian (2010) highlights, modern information systems rely on a substantial physical backbone that enables organizations to create and share knowledge effectively.

Ecological responsibility is inseparable from technological progress. Chip fabrication depends on fragile mineral supply chains. Data centers require water and power. Global logistics affect real communities. A responsible AI ecosystem must include an assessment of the feasibility of building, what building entails, and who bears the implicit and explicit costs. These issues carry ethical implications that shape the trajectory of AI.

Within organizations, physical capital continually interacts with human, structural, and intellectual capital. Tools, labs, workshops, and digital platforms shape how people think, collaborate, and learn. They invite discovery, channel attention, and foster habits of renewal. Well-designed environments align with the routines and expectations of structural capital (Stewart 1997; Roos et al. 1997). An ecological posture also recognizes that the earth itself is not an expendable infrastructure. It is the shared home within which human, intellectual, and technological capital must operate responsibly. Physical capital is the kinetic element of the capital system and requires ethical stewardship.

SIDEBAR 1.4   PHYSICAL CAPITAL: MATTER, MACHINES, AND THE EARTH WE DEPEND ON

What physical capital includes
- buildings, laboratories, workshops, classrooms, and clinics
- machines, tools, vehicles, networks, and digital infrastructure
- prototypes, testing environments, and experimental equipment
- the natural world, including land, water, air, minerals, forests, and ecosystems

Why it matters
- turns ideas into reality
- enables experimentation, repair, and refinement
- shapes how people work, collaborate, and learn
- determines whether innovation becomes sustainable or extractive
- comprises the environment on which life depends

AI and Physical Reality

AI is not virtual; it requires physical presence:
- chips and fabrication facilities
- data centers, cooling systems, and power grids
- minerals, manufacturing supply chains, and water
- communities that host and live near the infrastructure

Responsible AI requires attention to algorithms, data, and the material footprint.

Guiding principle. Steward physical capital with the future in mind because people, organizations, and societies will depend on it. The creation and use of physical capital are intergenerational concerns.

Financial Capital

Financial capital is the form of capital most people think of when they hear the word capital. It is empowering, leverageable, and evokes images of wealth. Without it, the ability to mobilize resources, mitigate risk, attract talent, and sustain productive human activity is sharply limited. Financial capital includes money, credit, equity, debt instruments, cash reserves, and reliable cash flows that enable individuals, organizations, and societies to start, grow, stabilize, and renew productive work. It is the financial lifeblood that supports investment, learning, and the conversion of ideas into tangible outcomes.

Economic and organizational research has long shown that access to financial capital shapes societies' ability to innovate, adapt, and generate new knowledge. From early development and growth theory to contemporary financial economics, scholars demonstrate that financial resources enable investments in human, physical, and all forms of capital, strengthening productivity and fostering technological progress (Schumpeter 1980; King and Levine 1993; Levine 1997). Well-structured financial systems also reduce transaction costs, distribute risk more effectively, and improve capital allocation, creating environments where creativity and discovery can flourish rather than collapse under pressure (Greenwood and Jovanovic 1990; Rajan and Zingales 1998).

Cash flow is central to capital stability and mission sustainability. It shows whether an organization or society can meet obligations, care for people, and weather periods of uncertainty. Healthy, disciplined cash flow sustains the mission. Unpredictable or negative cash flow erodes trust, forces short-term decision-making, and eventually weakens every other form of capital. Credit and cash flow are partners. Credit smooths periods of uneven cash flow, but ultimately, cash flow repays creditors.

The connection between financial capital and AI makes clear the interdependent relationships among capital, mission, and operational sustainability. Building AI systems requires significant up-front investment: computing and data infrastructure, cloud systems, engineering teams, and extended periods of experimentation and refinement. These commitments often occur years before meaningful revenue appears and depend on both financial capital and reliable cash flow to absorb risk and support learning. AI is not merely software. It is an investment in predictive capacity, institutional competence, and organizational credibility, all of which require sustained financial commitment (Agrawal, Gans, and Goldfarb 2018; Brynjolfsson and McAfee 2016).

Venture capital, financial engineering, and private equity often serve as catalysts. They take early risk, fund experimentation, expand capital and risk pools, and nurture ideas that traditional financing may overlook. Properly stewarded, financial capital serves as both a buffer and an accelerator. It creates space for trial and error, supports patient discovery, and helps promising innovations mature rather than collapse under short-term financial pressure (Gompers and Lerner 2001[1]; Kortum and Lerner 2000[2]).

Financial capital is not merely liquidity or accounting value. It is the strategic resource that connects human, physical, intellectual, and structural capital, enabling their ethical development and interaction. As AI continues reshaping economies, financial capital, including thoughtful attention to cash-flow discipline, becomes even more essential. It helps carry the high fixed costs, long development cycles, and repeated adjustments needed to transform technological potential into genuine human flourishing.

SIDEBAR 1.5   FOUNDATIONS OF FINANCIAL CAPITAL AND AI

Irving Fisher: time, value, and risk. Fisher linked interest, present value, and intertemporal choice, showing how financial capital moves value across time and enables investment and savings (Fisher 1930).

AI relevance: AI sharpens forecasting, improves risk assessment, and helps evaluate trade-offs over time. AI also requires intertemporal financial forbearance for development and deployment.

Modigliani and Miller: capital structure. Modigliani and Miller showed how capital structure affects risk, returns, and the cost of financing (Modigliani and Miller 1958, 1963).

AI relevance: AI improves stress testing, scenario modeling, and capital-structure planning.

Robert Merton: managing risk. Merton extended financial theory to dynamic environments where risk can be transferred, hedged, and insured (Merton 1995, 1998).

AI relevance: AI enhances real-time hedging strategies and systemic-risk monitoring. AI development, refinement, and deployment require risk hedging and risk transfer, including the use of special-purpose vehicles and other financial engineering techniques.

Joseph Stiglitz: imperfect information. Stiglitz showed that real markets operate under uncertainty and asymmetric information (Stiglitz 2000).

AI relevance: AI reduces inevitable information disparities while also creating new asymmetries in data access and in transparency around algorithms and data.

Why cash flow matters. Cash flow sustains operations, protects the mission during periods of uncertainty, and enables organizations to invest patiently in people, infrastructure, learning, and innovation. Without disciplined cash flow, financial capital is vulnerable to speculation rather than constructive investment.

Synthesis. Financial capital enables investment, growth, and value creation. AI strengthens these functions by expanding access to information, improving risk management, and refining allocation decisions, but only when guided by prudence, transparency, and ethical intent. The creation, development, and use of AI depend on financial capital.

Ethical Capital

Ethical capital comprises higher purposes that guide individual, social, and organizational judgments, decisions, choices, and structures toward justice, responsibility, societal well-being, care for the natural world, and the flourishing of human life. It shapes how people and institutions understand what is right, permissible, and worth doing. Some argue that laws, regulations, and other elements of structural capital are sufficient to address ethical concerns. Yet, formal systems often offer limited ethical governance controls.

Legal frameworks tend to be reactive and slow. Courts may take years to resolve disputes over technologies, products, or practices, and even successful legal outcomes can leave communities dissatisfied or insufficiently compensated (Raworth 2017; Sen 2011).[3] Structural capital alone cannot guarantee fairness, sustainability, or long-term benefit when technologies are misused, structures lack ethical alignment, or harm occurs outside the narrow legal boundaries.

Ethical capital addresses this gap by working upstream. It cultivates virtues, habits, and expectations that prevent abuse before it occurs. Ethical capital sharpens moral instincts. It trains and moves leaders and organizations beyond the 'can we do this' question to the 'should we do this' question. Ethical capital clarifies what an action means for people, communities, and the natural world. It fosters responsibility, transparency, fairness, inclusion, ecological stewardship, and long-term thinking, strengthening society, the environment, and human thriving.

At the same time, ethical capital plays a decisive role in organizational and societal reputation. Reputation is not merely image management. It is the accumulated public judgment of whether organizations and individuals can be trusted to act responsibly and in line with their stated purposes. Strong ethical capital attracts employees, investors, students, customers, donors, partners, and citizens who want to participate in organizations and with individuals they believe are credible and just (Freeman et al. 2010; Edmans 2020). Weak ethical capital repels them.

In this sense, ethical capital becomes a growth engine. It reduces ambiguity, lowers risk, and builds confidence that commitments will be honored. Stakeholders, those with a vested interest in an organization's or society's activities and outcomes, extend trust more freely, collaboration becomes easier, and the other forms of capital, including human, intellectual, structural, physical, and financial capital, can expand within a stable ethical framework (Freeman et al. 2010).

AI intensifies the need for mature ethical capital. As AI increasingly functions as intellectual capital, scaling knowledge, automating decisions, and amplifying human capability, it also magnifies risks of bias, surveillance, lack of transparency, misinformation, and misuse (Floridi and Cowls 2019).[4] Ethical capital sets the boundaries within which AI remains human centered and life affirming. Ethical capital serves as the integrating force and the glue of the capital system. It aligns the other forms of capital along a virtuous path:

- stabilizes human capital through trustworthy formation

- guides intellectual capital toward truth and responsible use

- shapes structural capital toward justice

- disciplines financial capital away from economic extraction and toward long-term value

- directs physical and technological capital toward sustainability and stewardship

Without ethical capital, the other forms of capital fragment, compete, or exploit one another—the total stock of capital decays. With ethical capital, capital aligns and converges toward a coherent purpose, shared flourishing, and sustainable growth.

SIDEBAR 1.6   ETHICAL CAPITAL, REPUTATION, AND CAPITAL ALIGNMENT

Short definition. Ethical capital is the traditions, values, virtues, and shared commitments that guide behavior toward the common good. It builds credibility, reputation, and social legitimacy (Freeman et al. 2010; Edmans 2020).

Why it matters
- prevents harm before it occurs
- builds sustained trust and reputation
- attracts stakeholders and partners
- reduces risk and strengthens legitimacy
- aligns choices with long-term well-being

The law is not enough. Legal systems respond after harm occurs and cannot anticipate every situation (Sen 2011; Raworth 2017). Ethical capital broadens the moral horizon, enabling organizations to choose what is right rather than merely what is legal.

AI connection. AI increases capability and the consequences. Ethical capital recognizes shared boundaries, protects dignity, demands accountability, and resists bias and manipulation (Floridi and Cowls 2019).

The integrating force. Ethical capital is the glue that holds the capital system together. It aligns human, intellectual, structural, physical, and financial capital toward sustainability, societal well-being, and human flourishing.

Human beings remain the agents who shape how capital is formed, aligned, and used. Table 1.1 summarizes how human capital interacts with the complementary forms of capital that support it.

TABLE 1.1   Interaction of Human Capital with the Five Complementary Forms of Capital

Form of Capital	Core Definition	How It Interacts With Human Capital
Intellectual Capital	Explicit knowledge, expertise, algorithms, models, recorded innovations, and repositories of ideas that extend reasoning and problem-solving.	Enhances the analytical, creative, and decision capacities of human capital, and provides tools and conceptual frameworks that amplify skilled judgment and discovery.
Structural Capital	Systems, processes, institutions, organizational routines, and governance infrastructures that persist beyond individuals.	Channels human capital by providing stable platforms for action, reduces complexity, and enables individuals to contribute more effectively within coordinated systems.
Physical Capital	Tangible assets such as tools, machines, technologies, built environments, and nature.	Extends the physical and operational reach of human abilities, and increases productivity, precision, and scale of human effort.
Financial Capital	Monetary resources, investments, and funding structures that enable the acquisition and deployment of other forms of capital.	Provides the means for developing, sustaining, and expanding human capital through education, training, health, and professional development.
Ethical Capital	Traditions, shared experiences, and expectations that guide virtuous and sustainable behaviors and support social cohesion.	Shapes the responsible use of human capital and action, and creates environments that reward integrity, collaboration, care, and long-term flourishing.

The six forms of capital do not operate in isolation. They mature and decay together. Human insight generates knowledge. Knowledge shapes institutions. Institutions mobilize and guide resources. Resources require financing and direction. All of this must be guided by ethical purpose. When technology, including AI, alters one form of capital, the effects ripple through the others. Recognizing these interactions helps individuals and leaders see that progress is never merely technical or financial. Progress is always human, relational, moral, and profoundly shaped by the choices we make about how capital is cultivated and used.

A BRIEF SCAN OF CAPITAL TRANSFORMATION

When Johannes Gutenberg introduced movable-type printing in the fifteenth century, he transformed intellectual capital and, with it, human development. Knowledge once confined to monasteries became widely accessible (Dawson 1991). Literacy spread, reshaping human capital, weakening centralized authority, and sparking cultural renewal (Febvre and Martin 2010). As literacy became an essential economic skill, markets adapted. Publishing and education expanded, and human capital grew beyond caste and clerical boundaries, paving the way for broad cultural change.

The steam engine and nineteenth-century railroads transformed physical capital by compressing time and distance. They also reshaped labor markets, financial flows, and the spatial layout of cities (Schivelbusch 2014). Financial markets expanded to support infrastructure. Insurance and banking became more sophisticated, and national financial networks emerged, enabling regional integration.

By the late nineteenth and early twentieth centuries, a new form of extractive capitalism had taken shape—extractive in the sense that value creation and value retention became increasingly decoupled. A narrow set of actors captured disproportionate returns from the collective human capital of many contributors (Acemoglu and Robinson 2013). Productivity was increasingly measured by return on capital, leverage, and efficiency metrics that separated labor from its rewards. Accumulation displaced reciprocity, and stewardship gave way to extraction (Piketty 2014; Polanyi 2001).

The twentieth century's agricultural revolution likewise redefined multiple forms of capital. Synthetic fertilizers, pesticides, hybrid seeds, and genetically modified organisms increased food production but depleted natural systems and created new dependencies (Shiva 2016). Food systems became centralized, and increased productivity reduced labor requirements. These changes exposed the interdependence of human, physical, and ethical capital.

Hydroelectric development through the Tennessee Valley Authority illustrates how capital can be mobilized quickly. Dams and power grids transformed physical capital. Engineering innovation expanded human and intellectual capital. At the same time, sacred lands were flooded and communities displaced, weakening ethical capital and cultural continuity (Hargrove 1994).

Automobiles restructured labor, communities, and geography. Assembly lines defined employment. Suburbs and highways remade landscapes. Financial markets grew around auto loans and oil futures. At the same time, automation displaced workers even as physical infrastructure expanded (Sugrue 2005).

The Internet, like the printing press before it, revolutionized intellectual capital. Knowledge became widely distributed and rapidly accessible. Yet, digital platforms also monetize attention, centralize control, and accelerate distraction. Local journalism weakened, and disinformation eroded both ethical and intellectual capital (Zuboff 2019).

Cycles of Consolidation and Renewal

Across these transformations, societies have experienced recurring cycles of concentration, disruption, adaptation, and renewal. Joseph Schumpeter (1942) described this pattern as creative destruction, in which old structures give way to new forms of growth. Clayton Christensen (1997) later showed that disruptive entrants challenge incumbents not by competing directly but by reframing value and redefining the rules of participation.

AI fits within this pattern of technological change and disruption. Its influence cannot be understood apart from the six forms of capital it touches. AI can expand capability, deepen knowledge, and support coordination. It can also intensify inequality, accelerate extraction, or erode trust when misaligned with ethical purpose. Technology reflects the cultures and values that shape it. If AI is to serve humanity, it must be guided by conscience, wisdom, and care. The goal is not simply to build more intelligent machines. It is to form wiser people who govern powerful tools responsibly.

Capital tells a story of human possibility. The six forms of capital remind us that progress is never only technical or financial. It is relational, moral, educational, and deeply human. When capital is aligned, societies develop capacity, resilience, and purpose. When it becomes distorted, accumulation replaces stewardship, extraction outruns renewal, and people are left behind.

AI shapes this capital and social landscape as an extension of intellectual and structural power. It amplifies what already exists. Where capital systems are healthy, AI can deepen learning, coordination, and discovery. Where capital systems are weak or unjust, AI can accelerate inequity, concentrate control, amplify extraction, and erode trust.

The path forward is not only about designing better systems. It is about forming wiser communities and cultivating more thoughtful leaders. It is about crafting ethical capital strong enough to guide invention, human capital capable of discernment, and organizations where stakeholders remember why they exist. When capital is used effectively to advance human flourishing, the natural world, sustainable organizations, and healthy communities, technological power serves rather than dominates.

AI engages each form of capital not as an inevitable force but as a mirror that reflects prevailing priorities, neglected responsibilities, and emerging trajectories of character and purpose. Human agency remains decisive. It determines how, when, and why AI is employed, and whether it functions as constructive intellectual capital that strengthens human life, the natural world, organizational integrity, and societal well-being.

TAKEAWAYS

- Capital is never only financial. It is human, intellectual, structural, physical, ethical, and relational.

- Each form of capital grows stronger when it upholds dignity, the natural world, and the flourishing of people, society, and communities.

- Human beings possess agency. People decide how capital is formed, aligned, and used.

- Technologies, including AI, do not create purpose. They reveal and amplify existing purposes.

- When capital systems drift toward extraction, power, and control, technology amplifies harm and accelerates inequities.

- The future of AI depends less on what machines can do and more on the people and organizations that shape AI's use, development, and deployment.

NOTES

1 Paul A. Gompers and Josh Lerner, "The Venture Capital Revolution," *Journal of Economic Perspectives* 15, no. 2 (2001): 145–168. Venture capital provides liquidity, governance support, and disciplined risk-taking for young firms operating under uncertainty, particularly in technology sectors such as AI.

2 Samuel Kortum and Josh Lerner, "Assessing the Contribution of Venture Capital to Innovation," *RAND Journal of Economics* 31, no. 4 (2000): 674–692. Industries receiving greater venture funding produced significantly higher rates of patented innovation, underscoring the catalytic role of financial systems in technological development.

3 Kate Raworth, *Doughnut Economics: Seven Ways to Think Like a 21st-Century Economist* (White River Junction, VT: Chelsea Green Publishing, 2017). Raworth proposes economic systems designed to be regenerative and distributive, a framework in which AI may broaden access, participation, and ethical awareness.

4 Luciano Floridi and Josh Cowls, "A Unified Framework of Five Principles for AI in Society," *Harvard Data Science Review* 1, no. 1 (2019). https://doi.org/10.1162/99608f92.8cd550d1. The authors synthesize global AI ethics frameworks into five principles, highlighting explicability as essential for intelligibility and accountability in AI governance.

WORKS CITED

Acemoglu, Daron, and James A. Robinson. 2013. *Why Nations Fail: The Origins of Power, Prosperity and Poverty*. New York: Crown Currency.

Agrawal, Ajay, Joshua Gans, and Avi Goldfarb. 2018. *Prediction Machines: The Simple Economics of Artificial Intelligence*. Cambridge: Harvard Business Review Press.

Arendt, Hannah. 1998. *The Human Condition* (2nd ed.). Chicago: The University of Chicago Press.

Becker, Gary S. 1994. *Human Capital: A Theoretical and Empirical Analysis with Special Reference to Education* (3rd ed.). Chicago: University of Chicago Press.

Bourdieu, Pierre. 2021. *Forms of Capital: General Sociology* (1st ed., Vol. 3). Hoboken, NJ: Polity.

Brynjolfsson, Erik, and Andrew McAfee. 2016. *The Second Machine Age: Work, Progress, and Prosperity in a Time of Brilliant Technologies*. New York: W. W. Norton & Company.

Brynjolfsson, Erik, and Tom Mitchell. 2017. "What Can Machine Learning Do?" *Science* 358 (6370): 1530–1534.

Brynjolfsson, Erik, Daniel Rock, and Chad Syverson. 2017. *Artificial Intelligence and the Modern Productivity Paradox: A Clash of Expectations and Statistics*. Working Paper 24001. Cambridge, MA: National Bureau of Economic Research.

Christensen, Clayton M. 1997. *The Innovator's Dilemma: When New Technologies Cause Great Firms to Fail*. Boston: Harvard Business School Press.

Davenport, Thomas H. 1999. *Human Capital: What It Is and Why People Invest It*. San Francisco, CA: Jossey-Bass.

Davenport, Thomas H., and Lawrence Prusak. 2000. *Working Knowledge; How Organizations Manage What They Know*. Boston: Harvard Business School Press.

Davenport, Thomas H., and Rajeev Ronanki. 2018, January–February. "Artificial Intelligence for the Real World." *Harvard Business Review Magazine*.

Dawson, Christopher. 1991. *Religion and the Rise of Western Culture: The Classic Study of Medieval Civilization* (Abridged ed.). New York: The Crown Publishing Group.

Edmans, Alex. 2020. *Grow the Pie: How Great Companies Deliver Both Purpose and Profit*. Cambridge: Cambridge University Press.

Febvre, Lucien, and Henri-Jean Martin. 2010. *The Coming of the Book: The Impact of Printing 1450-1800*. London: Verso Books.

Felin, Teppo, and Matthias Holweg. 2024, February 24. "Theory Is All You Need: AI, Human Cognition, and Causal Reasoning." *Strategy Science* 9 (4): 346–371.

Fisher, Irving. 1930. *The Theory of Interest*. New York: The Macmillan Company.

Floridi, Luciano, and Josh Cowls. 2019, Summer. "A Unified Framework of Five Principles for AI in Society." *Harvard Data Science Review* 1 (1). doi: 10.1162/99608f92.8cd550d1

Freeman, Edward, Jeffrey S. Harrison, Andrew C. Wicks, Bidhan L. Palmer, and Simone de Colle. 2010. *Stakeholder Theory: The State of the Art*. Cambridge: Cambridge University Press.

Gompers, Paul A., and Josh Lerner. 2001. "The Venture Capital Revolution." *Journal of Economic Perspectives* 15 (2): 145–168.

Greenwood, Jeremy, and Boyan Jovanovic. 1990. "Financial Development, Growth, and the Distribution of Income." *Journal of Political Economy* 98 (5 Part 1): 1076–1107.

Hargrove, Edwin C. 1994. *Prisoners of Myth: The Leadership of the Tennessee Valley Authority, 1933-1990*. Princeton: Princeton University Press.

Hippel, Eric Von. 2006. *Democratizing Innovation*. Cambridge, MA: The MIT Press.

Jorgenson, Dale W. 1963. "Capital Theory and Investment Behavior." *American Economic Review* 53 (2): 247–259.

King, Robert G., and Ross Levine. 1993. "Finance and Growth: Schumpeter Might Be Right." *Quarterly Journal of Economics* 108 (3): 727–737.

Kortum, Samuel, and Josh Lerner. 2000. "Assessing the Contribution of Venture Capital to Innovation." *The RAND Journal of Economics* 31 (4): 674–692.

Levine, Ross. 1997. "Financial Development and Economic Growth: Views and Agenda." *Journal of Economic Literature* 35 (2): 688–726.

MacIntyre, Alasdair C. 1981. *After Virtue: A Study in Moral Theory*. South Bend: University of Notre Dame Press.

Merton, Robert C. 1995, June. "Financial Innovation and the Management and Regulation of Financial Institutions." *Journal of Banking & Finance* 19 (3–4): 461–481.

Merton, Robert C. 1998, June. "Applications of Option-Pricing Theory: Twenty-Five Years Later." *The American Economic Review* 88 (3): 323–349.

Mincer, Jacob. 1974. *Schooling, Experience, and Earnings*. New York: NBER.

Modigliani, Franco, and Merton H. Miller. 1958, June. "The Cost of Capital, Corporation Finance and the Theory of Investment." *The American Economic Review* 48 (3): 261–297.

Modigliani, Franco, and Merton H. Miller. 1963, June. "Corporate Income Taxes and the Cost of Capital: A Correction." *The American Economic Review* 53 (3): 433–443.

Piketty, Thomas. 2014. *Capital in the Twenty-First Century*. Translated by Arthur Goldhammer. Cambridge: Belknap Press.

Polanyi, Karl. 2001. *The Great Transformation: The Political and Economic Origins of Our Time* (2nd ed.). Boston: Beacon Press.

Polanyi, Michael. 2019. *The Tacit Dimension*. Chicago: The University of Chicago Press.

Quinn, James Brian, Philip Anderson, and Sydney Finkelstein. 1996, March–April. "Managing Professional Intellect: Making the Most of the Best." *Harvard Business Review* 74 (2): 71–80.

Rajan, Raghuram G., and Luigi Zingales. 1998. "Financial Dependence and Growth." *American Economic Review* 88 (3): 559–586.

Raworth, Kate. 2017. *Doughnut Economics: Seven Ways to Think Like a 21st-Century Economist*. White River Junction, VT: Chelsea Green Publishing.

Roos, Goran, and Johan Roos. 1997, June. "Measuring Your Company's Intellectual Performance." *Long Range Planning* 30 (3): 413–426.

Roos, Johan, Goran Roos, Leif Edvinsson, and Nicola Dragonetti. 1997. *Intellectual Capital: Navigating in the New Business Landscape*. London: Palgrave Macmillan.

Rosenberg, Nathan. 1983. *Inside the Black Box: Technology and Economics*. Cambridge: Cambridge University Press.

Schivelbusch, Wolfgang. 2014. *The Railway Journey: The Industrialization of Time and Space in the Nineteenth Century* (1st ed.). Berkeley: University of California Press.

Schultz, Theodore W. 1961, March. "Investment in Human Capital." *The American Economic Review* 51 (1): 1–17.

Schumpeter, Joseph A. 1942. *Capitalism, Socialism, and Democracy*. New York: Harper & Brothers.

Schumpeter, Joseph A. 1980. *The Theory of Economic Development*. New Brunswick: Routledge.

Sen, Amartya. 2011. *The Idea of Justice*. Cambridge: Belknap Press.

Shiva, Vandana. 2016. *Who Really Feeds the World?: The Failures of Agribusiness and the Promise of Agroecology*. Berkeley, CA: North Atlantic Books.

Solow, Robert M. 1956. "A Contribution to the Theory of Economic Growth." *Quarterly Journal of Economics* 70 (1): 65–94.

Stewart, Thomas A. 1997. *Intellectual Capital: The New Wealth of Organizations*. New York: Currency.

Stiglitz, Joseph. 2000. "The Contributions of the Economics of Information to Twentieth Century Economics." *The Quarterly Journal of Economics* 115 (4): 1441–1478.

Sugrue, Thomas J. 2005. *The Origins of the Urban Crisis: Race and Inequality in Postwar Detroit*. Princeton: Princeton University Press.

Taylor, Charles. 1992. *Sources of the Self: The Makings of the Modern Identity*. Cambridge: Harvard University Press.

Teece, David J. 1986. "Profiting from Technological Innovation: Implications for Integration, Collaboration, Licensing, and Public Policy." *Research Policy* 15 (6): 285–305.

Varian, Hal. 2010. "Computer Mediated Transactions." *American Economic Review* 100 (2): 1–10.

Varian, Hal. 2018, July. *Artificial Intelligence, Economics, and Industrial Organization.* Accessed January 13, 2026, from NBER: https://www.nber.org/system/files/working_papers/w24839/w24839.pdf

Zuboff, Shoshana. 2019. *The Age of Surveillance Capitalism: The Fight for a Human Future at the New Frontier of Power.* New York: Public Affairs.

CHAPTER 2

The Balancing Act

AI, Society, and Capital Architecture

AI: A STRUCTURED INTELLECTUAL BUILDING BLOCK

Artificial intelligence (AI) is best understood as a building block and an accelerant of intellectual capital. It operates as part of the capital structure within the broader social architecture. Humans are the architects, society serves as the overall blueprint, and capital represents the structures that emerge from that blueprint, highlighting how organizations and societies responsibly balance capability and authority. AI influences outcomes through its architected integration with human, ethical, structural, physical, and financial capital. Its organizational and social consequences arise from how these forms of capital are designed, aligned, and governed rather than from the technology alone.

Public discussion too often emphasizes the apparent intelligence of AI-driven systems, yet this focus obscures a more consequential dynamic. AI reshapes environments rather than replacing human agency. It offers the architect more blueprint options and enhanced building materials, ultimately influencing how choices are structured, how information flows, and how power is distributed across institutions. Viewed through the lens of capital theory, AI operates as a mechanism of leverage that amplifies human intention. Its effects reflect the maturity, coherence, and governance quality of the capital architecture into which it is introduced.

There is precedent for this capital-architectural view of how AI affects all other forms of capital. In the eighteenth century, Adam Smith observed

DOI: 10.1201/9781003744061-2

that tools extend the productive powers of labor by embedding accumulated knowledge in material and procedural forms (Smith 1977). Subsequent scholars refined and extended this insight. Alfred Marshall (1890) identified knowledge as the most powerful engine of production. Fritz Machlup (1973) traced the emergence of knowledge industries and the economic consequences of organized knowledge production. Thomas Stewart (1997) argued that intellectual capital, rather than physical plant or labor alone, had become the principal source of leverage for creating value in modern organizations. Across these traditions, technology appears not as an autonomous force but as a lever of capital that channels human insight, or knowledge, into capital formation, which then reshapes that capital tool.

Some observers suggest that AI represents a fundamentally new form of intellectual capital because it can be trained, updated, and refined. This conclusion confuses adaptation with agency. The defining characteristic of intellectual capital has never been static knowledge, but rather its capacity for multiplication and adaptation. Intellectual capital grows by building on human insight, broad inquiry, accumulated capital, enhanced access, and new interpretations.

New research yields journal articles that provoke debate. Books synthesize ideas that reshape fields of study. Theories generate counterarguments, refinements, and entirely new lines of inquiry. The Internet and AI-enabled technologies expand access to knowledge. Each contribution broadens access to expertise and stimulates further creation, feeding both human development and the continual renewal of intellectual capital. This generative cycle is not accidental. It is the essence of intellectual capital, which exists to be expanded through human judgment, curiosity, imagination, and responsibility rather than to operate statically and independently.

Technology as a Lever of Human Capability

Every major technological transition, from the mechanical loom to the modern computer, follows a recognizable pattern. While the specific tools differ, the underlying dynamics remain remarkably consistent across historical periods and industries.

First, technology produces amplification. Human beings can accomplish more with less effort, time, or material input. Second, enhanced human productivity, innovation, and invention accelerate capital growth. Tasks that once required hours or days are compressed into minutes or seconds. Third, abstraction occurs as human work shifts from direct manual execution toward supervisory, interpretive, and integrative roles. Fourth, optimization occurs as industries reorganize workflows, skill requirements, and performance expectations to align with new technological capabilities. Finally, a next generation emerges when advances built on the previous technology initiate a new trajectory of change, repeating the cycle at a higher level of complexity.

These cyclic shifts are not accidental byproducts of innovation. They reflect the intent and growth of capital as a lever. Economists describe this pattern as the productivity function of capital, the capacity of a non-human bound asset to increase the output of human effort while reshaping economic incentives and organizational behavior (Solow 1956; Romer 1990).[1] Capital does not merely add capacity. It reshapes the social blueprint, affecting how life is lived, how work is performed, how effort is valued, and how capital is coordinated.

As technological systems mature, they consistently reduce time-on-task, staffing, material requirements, and the rework needed to achieve comparable or superior outcomes. This reflects a long-standing principle of economic innovation. As capital grows and is properly aligned (capital deepening), time, space, and material requirements compress. Capital deepening increases productivity by embedding more knowledge, precision, and capability in tools and processes. AI represents capital deepening at the intellectual level, extending analytical routines, pattern recognition, and embedded reasoning. The result is leverage, enabling individuals, organizations, and society to operate with expanded reach, speed, and complexity.

Economic and Social Consequences of Optimization

Technological optimization always produces systemic consequences. AI is no exception. As capital becomes more powerful and more deeply embedded in systems, human roles, skill profiles, and institutional structures must adapt. When this adaptation is not coordinated, well understood, and intentional, AI implementation can generate distortions alongside efficiency gains. These distortions are the unintended consequences of inconsistent capital planning and architecture.

One consequence is skill distillation. Expertise becomes concentrated among fewer workers who design, supervise, and interpret increasingly complex systems, while routine or intermediary tasks are compressed or eliminated. A second effect is employment dislocation, not only through changes in job quantity but also through shifts in job composition, particularly in entry- and mid-skill roles that are most exposed to automation and task restructuring (Autor et al. 2022). A third consequence is industrial disruption. Entire sectors reorganize around AI-enabled efficiencies, altering supply chains, competitive dynamics, and barriers to entry. A fourth effect involves shifts in capital returns that lead to a more concentrated pool of human capital, as value creation moves away from direct labor inputs and toward intellectual assets that scale more readily across organizations.

In organizations and societies where AI is effectively employed, a smaller but more capable base of human capital is amplified by returns on intellectual capital that flow back to its human implementers. Some fear that organizational optimization through AI will render some people and organizations obsolete. This fear belies a misunderstanding of the basic economic equation facing the world: unlimited needs and limited resources. These AI implementations can expand the efficacy of limited resources, allowing a smaller pool of human capital to leverage capital more effectively to meet the world's unlimited needs.

Joseph Schumpeter (1942) captured this process as creative destruction, in which new combinations of capital reorganize production; old institutional arrangements lose economic viability; innovation reshapes incentives, authority, and returns; and value is both created and eroded simultaneously. Schumpeter saw technology as the instrument, not the agent, of this creative-destructive process. AI will ultimately, through the creative destruction process, create new economic horizons, but there will be painful shifts in the institutional and human gears of society and organizations. Understanding the social and capital-architectural process determines the extent of that pain. Insightful and ethical leadership can not only dampen the pain but also redesign the blueprint to achieve new levels of human and organizational flourishing.

This leadership dynamic reflects a capital calculus rather than a zero-sum logic. Capital grows through intentional investment and alignment, not substitution. The successful story of capital growth and improvement is one in which humans flourish alongside these gains. Displacement requires investment in human capital to create new opportunities. Efficiencies require capital leverage rather than human leveraging. Upskilling requires time, patience, and investment.

AI AS A FORCE FOR FLOURISHING

AI development and deployments should be designed to strengthen all forms of capital. In healthcare, machine learning tools assist clinicians in early disease detection, improve diagnostic accuracy, and support treatment planning without displacing clinical authority. Systems trained on medical imaging datasets can identify pathologies earlier than conventional screening in some domains, enabling intervention at stages where treatment is most effective (Topol 2019[2]; Esteva et al. 2017[3]). When used as decision support rather than decision replacement, AI reduces error rates and enhances professional judgment, enabling clinicians to focus on interpretation, communication, and empathy.

These capital gains are especially relevant in labor-intensive service sectors affected by Baumol's Cost Disease, where productivity growth lags because core services depend primarily on skilled human labor (Baumol 2013). In the past, technology improved service quality without necessarily reducing the time the service provider spent on the task. Research shows that administrative burdens and limited productivity growth in services contribute significantly to long-term cost pressures that resist traditional economic remedies (Sahni et al. 2024). AI-enabled diagnostic systems, automated triage tools, and decision-support models provide partial relief from Baumol's Cost Disease by increasing throughput without burdening the service provider, reducing administrative burdens, improving quality, and reducing the scope of tasks required of the service provider.

AI handles elements of the task that would otherwise require the provider's time. As David Autor (2015) illustrates, technologies that automate routine tasks allow labor to be reallocated toward higher-value activities rather than eliminating workers. Wages rise for roles that design, supervise, and integrate AI-enabled systems, while clerical, administrative, and transactional tasks are restructured or phased out. Human capital is reoriented toward high-skilled, value-added work rather than administrative distractions. As AI becomes more capable, more administrative, clerical, diagnostic, and analytical tasks will be automated. This shift represents a reallocation of capital, with intellectual capital taking on more tasks, allowing humans to focus on better-informed interpretation, judgment, and decision-making.

AI also serves as a catalytic tool in research and knowledge creation. Pattern-recognition systems analyze datasets at scales no human research team could process alone, accelerating discovery without replacing interpretation. In biochemistry, AI-enabled protein structure prediction has compressed years of laboratory experimentation into computable insights that guide human inquiry (Jumper et al. 2021). In the social sciences and economics, AI supports simulation, scenario analysis, and model testing while leaving meaning-making and judgment to researchers. Knowledge does not originate in systems; it emerges through human interpretation supported by intellectual infrastructure.

Creativity offers a parallel illustration. AI tools assist artists, designers, musicians, and writers by generating drafts, variations, and stylistic options. These systems expand creative possibilities without determining intent or meaning. As with earlier technologies such as photography or digital editing, creative authority remains human, while AI accelerates iteration and reduces production costs (McCormack et al. 2019). Protecting intellectual property, image rights, and human dignity remains essential as these tools spread across the creative industries.

There are also cautionary notes about AI and human and social flourishing. The same systems that enhance human flourishing can undermine it. Generative technologies enable deception, fraud, and manipulation at scale. Deepfakes, synthetic identities, and automated impersonation erode trust in visual and written evidence (Chesney and Citron 2019). When this occurs, AI no longer amplifies human capital but instead degrades ethical capital and undermines the institutional legitimacy of organizations and societies. The reputational consequences for organizations and AI can be severe and enduring. The human consequences can be devastating.

A subtler risk arises when judgment is deferred to systems. Automation bias arises not because AI is intelligent, but because authority is mistakenly attributed to it. When unchecked outputs and hallucinated responses replace critical evaluation, accountability erodes and skills decay (Parasuraman and Riley 1997; Floridi et al. 2018). The danger lies not in machines taking control, but in organizations and people relinquishing responsibility.

These new economic horizons and important cautions serve as reminders that humans are the architects. Rich and lasting architecture is achieved through the quality of decision-making and the choices made. Leaders of organizations, society, and individuals will decide AI's future—a future in which AI should be a multiplier of human capital.

SIDEBAR 2.1 AI AS A MULTIPLIER OF HUMAN CAPITAL

- AI does not generate value on its own. It amplifies and refines the value of human capabilities.
- When human capital development is substantial, AI amplifies judgment, creativity, and coordination. When human capital capability is weak, AI accelerates errors, dependency, and institutional fragility. This multiplier effect explains why identical technologies produce radically different outcomes across organizations and societies.
- AI reveals rather than replaces human capital. Its impact reflects the maturity of the capital environments into which it is introduced.

A solid design choice requires proper nomenclature and classification. AI is often mischaracterized as a form of synthetic intelligence. This description is technically inaccurate and carries significant governance implications. Even large-scale neural systems that generate fluent language or strategic recommendations do so through statistical inference rather than understanding (*Artificial Intelligence: A Modern Approach* 2021). As Luciano Floridi (2014a) observes, AI's appearance of intelligence reflects computational scale and performance rather than cognition, sentience, or intentional meaning.

When AI is treated as a human with agency, errors are framed as AI system failures rather than as failures of leadership and oversight. Decisions are attributed to model behavior rather than to organizational short-sightedness. This conceptual slippage erodes ethical capital by obscuring who bears responsibility for outcomes and who must answer for harm. AI, as a system, does not bear legal or moral accountability. Organizational and societal leaders do. AI does not assume responsibility. It reshapes where authority appears to reside, heightening the need for governance structures that preserve human accountability, transparency, and disciplined oversight.

Distinguishing AI's role from human agency is essential to avoid governance oversight issues. Meaning arises from the integration of emotion, memory, anticipation, narrative identity, and moral judgment (Damasio 2005; Baars 1988). Humans interpret experience, assign significance, and deliberate among values. AI performs none of these functions. AI extends intellectual capability by accelerating analysis and coordination.

SIDEBAR 2.2 GOVERNANCE FAILURES THAT ENABLE AI MISUSE

- AI does not fail on its own. It reflects the quality of the governance structures that guide it.
- Misuse arises when decision authority shifts from people to systems.
- Effective governance preserves human judgment, aligns optimization with the mission, and maintains transparency—ethical capital serves as the stabilizing framework.

ACCELERATION WITHOUT GOVERNANCE

John Maynard Keynes (1972) introduced the term 'technological unemployment' in 1930 to describe transitional disruptions that accompany capital deepening and scientific progress. More recently, Floridi (2014b) has emphasized that the most significant risks of acceleration fall not on society but on those whose livelihoods, skills, and opportunities are most exposed to rapid capital reconfiguration. Acceleration has human, social, economic, cultural, and governance consequences. The imperative, then, is to anticipate and structure capital shifts before technological implementations to provide a buffer.

Just as an organization would not buy software without hardware and training to implement it fully, a savvy organization or society should implement AI only after preparing the human and other forms of capital for its launch.

AI and Productivity Reconsidered

AI improves efficiency by adding intellectual firepower to organizations, accelerating their capacity to decide, coordinate, track, judge, and create (Brynjolfsson and McAfee 2016). Productivity, however, is not synonymous with speed or volume. The adage 'haste makes waste' applies equally to AI-driven systems. Effective productivity reflects systemwide value creation, which depends on the readiness of capital structures, ethical frameworks, and operational systems to sustain an accelerated and enriched pace. Research by Daron Acemoglu and Pascual Restrepo (2020) shows that technological automation contributes to sustained growth only when paired with workforce integration and human preparation.

When education, job redesign, and organizational reforms lag, AI implementation tends to replace rather than enhance employment. In such conditions, there is a real risk that essential human capital is removed before the full range of complementary capital is identified and developed. The result can be capital misalignment. AI then risks becoming a short-term extractive process in which capital is consumed for immediate gains rather than for capital regeneration. When introduced as an extractive form of capital, AI erodes rather than strengthens the underlying capital base.

SIDEBAR 2.3   EXTRACTIVE CAPITALISM: CORE CHARACTERISTICS[4]

- Extractive capitalism is an economic pattern in which value is generated by drawing down existing forms of capital rather than renewing or expanding them. Returns are prioritized in the short term, often by leveraging financial, physical, or intellectual assets without corresponding investment in human, structural, or ethical capital.
- Standard features of extractive systems include the concentration of decision-making authority, the compression or erosion of skill development, and the externalization of social and organizational costs. Efficiency gains may appear strong in the near term, but they are achieved by weakening the foundations that sustain long-term productivity, trust, and adaptability.
- In contrast, additive or regenerative capital systems reinvest gains in human capability, institutional learning, and ethical governance. Over time, these systems produce more resilient organizations and broader value creation. The distinction is not technological but institutional. The same tools can support either outcome, depending on how capital is governed, allocated, and renewed.

AI AND RISK: CAPITAL-SPECIFIC VULNERABILITIES

The risks associated with AI adoption do not arise uniformly across organizations or societies. They emerge where specific forms of capital are weak, misaligned, or insufficiently governed.

Education and Human Capital Risks

AI can expand access, enable adaptive learning, and reduce administrative burden in educational systems. However, education is not reducible to the transfer of information. It is the formation of judgment, self-direction, and intellectual discipline, which together constitute core elements of intellectual capital (Bruner 1990). AI can support instruction, assessment, and analytics, but it cannot substitute for mentorship, moral formation, or the cultivation of character. These dimensions of formation remain fundamentally human processes shaped by relationships with parents, teachers, mentors, and leaders (Bandura 1977). Empirical research consistently shows that AI technologies increase returns to abstract reasoning and judgment while reducing returns to routine tasks, reinforcing the central role of human formation in the development of value-creating intellectual capital (Autor 2015; Acemoglu and Restrepo 2020).

Knowledge and Operational Insight Risks

Intellectual capital comprises organized, explicit knowledge. AI converts portions of this knowledge into operational routines at scale. AI can significantly amplify this explicit knowledge, but when AI is deployed indiscriminately, human tacit knowledge, which comprises organizational know-how and know-why, can be lost, introducing a distinct risk of losing necessary organizational abilities.

Effective use of AI requires people with discipline, customer orientation, and deep mastery of their domain to understand what intellectual systems can legitimately offer, what to automate, and where human judgment must remain decisive. As Michael Polanyi (2019) famously observed, human beings know more than they can fully articulate—tacit knowledge. Excessive automation preserves outputs while quietly eroding understanding of the underlying causes. This loss of comprehension weakens the interpretive and diagnostic capacities that organizations depend on over time (Polanyi 2019; Zuboff 1989).

Structural, Physical, and Ethical Capital Risks

Structural capital comprises governance rules and practices. AI may increase consistency but may also embed assumptions that were not anticipated or intended (Eubanks 2018; Zuboff 2019). When this unanticipated embedding of governance occurs, leaders may be left with a false sense of security. Rules or embedded decisions are followed, but their results are unwarranted and unwelcome. AI's governance pathways must be explicit and frequently reviewed. Much like explicit structural capital, an organization's or society's use of physical capital should be intentional and designed to mitigate damage. AI's physical capital depends on data centers, energy systems, and semiconductor supply chains, introducing geopolitical and environmental risks (Goldfarb and Tucker 2019).

Ethical capital is the upstream source of social wisdom and shared values that organizational and societal leaders leverage to guide AI. When properly structured, ethical capital builds trust, reinforces legitimacy, and aligns capital with desired outcomes. These ethical foundations should be embedded within concrete governance architectures that operate across organizational, industry, national, and international levels. Without appropriate integration of ethical capital and robust governance, risks of reputational damage, legal entanglements, and loss of goodwill abound.

GOVERNANCE ARCHITECTURES, CAPITAL STRUCTURE, AND CAPITAL ALLOCATION

At the organizational level, governance is expressed through internal policies, incentive structures, audit mechanisms, and leadership accountability. Industry governance arises from professional standards, shared norms, and sector-specific codes of practice. National governance reflects legislative priorities, statutory law, regulatory capacity, and judicial enforcement. International governance advances more slowly through treaties, multilateral institutions, and soft-law frameworks designed to harmonize standards across borders. These layers do not operate independently. Together, they form a nested governance architecture that shapes how AI systems are designed, deployed, constrained, and legitimized.

Regulatory philosophies vary significantly across jurisdictions. European approaches emphasize precaution, risk classification, and the protection of human dignity, reflecting the European Union's rights-based regulatory tradition (European Union 2024). The United States prioritizes innovation, market competition, and decentralized oversight, relying heavily on ex post enforcement and sector-specific regulation. China maintains centralized government control, integrating AI governance into national planning, industrial policy, and security objectives (China 2023). None of these approaches is ethically neutral. Each carries implicit judgments about power, responsibility, acceptable risk, and the proper relationship among individuals, markets, and the state (Floridi et al. 2018; Acemoglu and Johnson 2023).

These governance choices directly shape societal and organizational capital structures and strongly influence how human capital is formed, deployed, and rewarded. Capital is not created by investment alone. Incentives sustain it. Human capital grows when education, judgment, and professional discretion are valued and rewarded. Intellectual and structural capital expand when institutions emphasize transparency, explainability, and long-term organizational learning. Intellectual property must be protected from misuse, or it deteriorates due to weakened incentives and declining creative investment. Ethical capital increases when legitimacy, trust, and restraint are valued and generate sustained gains. Conversely, when governance systems reward short-term extraction, secrecy, or unchecked growth, capital eventually erodes.

This risk–reward–incentive dynamic lies at the heart of capital theory. Capital grows or contracts in response to incentives and returns over time. All forms of capital expand in response to the rewards they generate. In market-based systems, markets do more than set prices; they also reflect societal priorities and values. Mission-based organizations' capital responds to rewards such as grants, donations, votes, and taxes. In both market-driven and mission-driven systems, capital enables organizations to respond to revealed needs. When returns are strong, capital grows and is strengthened. When returns weaken, capacity diminishes (Solow 1956; Piketty 2014). Governance, organizational performance, and ethical performance play a decisive role in capital formation by shaping how returns are recognized across different forms of capital.

Capital budgeting decisions translate governance and performance principles into operational reality. Capital budgeting is also a key architectural activity. Investing in AI systems is never merely a technical decision. Budgeting choices determine whether AI enhances human capability or substitutes for it, whether structural capital reinforces accountability or obscures responsibility, and whether ethical capital is strengthened through trust or depleted through coercion. Organizations that integrate ethical and governance considerations into budgeting and operations tend to experience more stable returns, lower risk exposure, and greater institutional legitimacy (Edmans 2011). Those who separate ethics from investment decisions may achieve short-term gains but often do so at the expense of long-term capital accretion.

Together, AI governance, capital structure, and capital budgeting form a continuous decision-making cycle. Governance defines acceptable ends. Capital structure signals what is rewarded. Capital budgeting executes those signals. AI does not disrupt this chain; it accelerates it, making visible whether institutions are investing in sustainable value creation or quietly drawing down the very capital foundations on which they depend.

SIDEBAR 2.4   CAPITAL BUDGETING IN A SIX-CAPITAL FRAMEWORK

Capital budgeting is the process by which organizations decide how to invest resources to generate future value. Traditionally, capital budgeting has focused on financial returns, using projected cash flows, discount rates, and risk-adjusted valuation. These tools remain necessary but are insufficient in environments shaped by AI, intangible assets, and long-term institutional responsibility. Within a six-capital model, capital budgeting serves as a governance function. It allocates incentives, authority, and attention across the multiple forms of capital.

- Human capital investments determine whether people gain skills, judgment, and professional discretion, or whether capability is substituted, narrowed, or allowed to erode (Becker 1994; Schultz 1961).
- Intellectual capital investments shape how knowledge is created, protected, made explicit, and reused, including whether learning compounds or stagnates over time (Stewart 1997; Roos et al. 1997).
- Structural capital investments embed governing assumptions into workflows, rules, and decision systems, determining whether accountability is reinforced through transparency or obscured by automation and a lack of transparency (North 1990; Eubanks 2018).
- Physical capital investment yields physical infrastructure, capacity, and environmental dependencies. Choices about energy use, data centers, hardware lifecycles, and supply chains directly affect sustainability outcomes and reputational risk. Environmental externalities increasingly shape regulatory exposure, stakeholder trust, and long-term operating costs, rather than remaining peripheral concerns (Goldfarb and Tucker 2019; Eccles, Ioannou, and Serafeim 2014).
- Financial capital investments allocate risk and reward, signaling which outcomes are valued and who benefits from success. Financial structure amplifies or constrains all other forms of capital but typically does not create value on its own (Modigliani and Miller 1958).

- Ethical capital investments define legitimacy, boundaries, and trust. Reputation is not merely symbolic. It governs stakeholder retention, including employees, customers, investors, and communities. Firms that sustain ethical capital experience greater loyalty, lower volatility, and more durable customer relationships, while ethical erosion accelerates disengagement and reputational loss (Edmans 2011; Porter and Kramer 2011; Zuboff 2019).

Every AI investment affects more than one form of capital. A system that increases efficiency may weaken judgment. A model that scales output may introduce environmental or reputational risk. Capital budgeting requires analyzing not only expected returns but also which forms of capital are strengthened, which are depleted, and over what time horizon.

Capital budgeting reveals priorities, but it does not create value on its own. Value emerges only when capital is directed, interpreted, and governed through wise human action.

HUMAN ACTION AND CAPITAL STRUCTURE

At the core of this capital and operational framework is human capability and action. The basis for sound action, including judgment, experience, creativity, discernment, and moral responsibility, resides entirely within people. All other forms of capital are created by human effort and respond to human discretion and action. Intellectual capital captures and extends knowledge, leading to informed action. Structural capital organizes action. Financial capital allocates resources to enable action. Physical capital provides infrastructure to support action. Ethical capital sustains trust and legitimacy through appropriate action. Purpose is grounded in human values and exercised through human choice expressed in action.

When capital is structured properly, each form of capital enables and informs human action. It is an upward movement of capability toward the top of the capital silo, or human capital that prepares people for action. When human capital, the endowment for action, is neglected or diminished, the hierarchy reverses. As judgment weakens, financial capital appears to dominate decision-making. As ethical formation declines, structural power becomes extractive rather than enabling. When competence erodes, technology is mythologized rather than governed. When accountability fades, intellectual systems are mistaken for sovereign rather than support. Capital was meant to serve people. When organizations and society prioritize things over people, they obscure the human role in value creation supported by capital. This distorts the natural capital hierarchy—capital was created for humans to flourish. Humans do not serve capital; capital serves humans. A distorted view of value creation shifts the source of value from humans to systems, finance, and other resources, eventually diminishing all forms of capital (Acemoglu and Robinson 2013; North 1990). AI is useful only when it rightly serves human needs and human flourishing.

CAPITAL BUDGETING IN THE AGE OF AI: STRATEGIC CAPITAL ARCHITECTURE

Capital budgeting in the age of AI should not be reduced to technology acquisition, cost reduction, or efficiency gains. Capital budgeting is the strategic architecture through which organizations and societies translate purpose into a sustainable, thriving form aligned with the needs of clients, citizens, and customers. It determines how different forms of capital are integrated, how authority and responsibility are distributed, and how human capability is cultivated over time. Whether the orientation is market based or mission driven, capital budgeting is the mechanism through which values become operational.

Traditional capital budgeting models often assume that assets generate returns directly. This assumption obscures the sources of value—human action. The central budgeting issue is not which technology to purchase, but which forms of capital to strengthen, how to align them, and toward what purpose.

As AI is integrated into the capital structure, it must also be architecturally integrated, engaging each form of capital deliberately and coherently. As AI capabilities expand, this architecture must be revisited and refined to ensure continued alignment with organizational purpose. The AI architecture must serve the organization's intellectual capital needs, whether market oriented, societal, or mission driven. AI's capital contribution and intended end purpose should be explicitly woven into the capital blueprint. AI's contribution to performance depends not on the technology itself but on the capital architecture within which it is embedded (Brynjolfsson and McAfee 2016; Acemoglu and Restrepo 2020).

Stakeholder Capital and Market Returns

Strategic capital architecture clarifies why stakeholder theory reshapes capital budgeting. Long-term value is created not by optimizing isolated inputs but by strengthening the entire capital ecosystem in which organizations operate. As Edward Freeman (2010) argues, firms achieve enduring performance when employees, customers, investors, communities, suppliers, and owners are seen as contributors to value creation rather than as constraints or mere considerations.

Empirical evidence supports this capital-architectural view. Firms that invest in human capability and ethical governance outperform peers over time, not through sentiment but through productivity, innovation, and reduced volatility. Alex Edmans (2011) shows that high employee satisfaction is associated with superior stock returns driven by operational performance rather than short-term signaling. Similarly, Robert Eccles, Ioannis Ioannou, and George Serafeim (2014) find that organizations with strong sustainability practices achieve better long-run performance due to lower risk exposure and higher stakeholder trust. Michael Porter and Mark Kramer (2011) emphasize that shared value emerges when social and economic goals are integrated rather than traded off.

Stakeholder-oriented capital budgeting also distinguishes financial structure from productive capability. Financial engineering may alter risk profiles and reported outcomes, but it does not create real, long-term value; it is a transactional strategy. Sustainable returns stem from skilled people, coherent institutions, and trusted governance. Organizations with weak human capital and exposed institutional legitimacy cannot engineer sustained advantage through leverage alone (Modigliani and Miller 1958; North 1990).

AI intensifies these dynamics. When AI strengthens skills, transparency, and governance, stakeholders reward organizations with capital, loyalty, and legitimacy. When AI obscures accountability or substitutes automated outputs for human judgment, trust erodes quietly before capital withdraws. Markets ultimately reward coherence, predictability, and sustainability rather than technical sophistication in isolation.

Hierarchy of Capital and Direction of Returns to Value Creation

When capital is well architected and governed, recognition of returns flows upward toward human capability. Returns are barometers of the quality of human capital, choices, and actions that arrange, develop, and leverage other forms of capital. When capital is misaligned or weak, return attribution flows downward into systems, assets, and financial extraction.

Figure 2.1 illustrates how returns move through the capital system. Ethical capital sets direction. Intellectual capital accelerates execution.

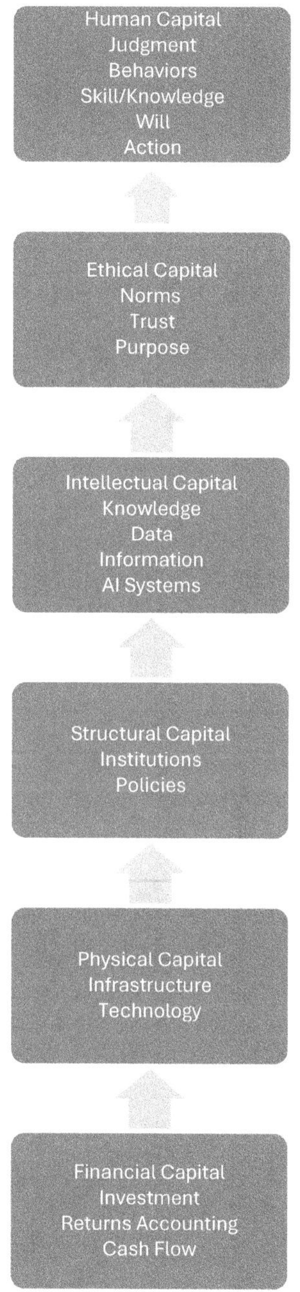

FIGURE 2.1 Capital hierarchy and returns to value creation.

Structural and physical capital channel governance and structural presence into practice. Financial capital distributes risk and reward. When this hierarchy is respected, returns compound upward, assessing and strengthening human capability, innovation, and trust.

Capital Structuring as Purpose

Capital budgeting is often treated as a financial allocation problem focused on project selection and efficiency. This view is incomplete. Properly understood, capital budgeting is the strategic architecture through which organizations and societies translate purpose into a sustainable, thriving form aligned with client, citizen, and customer needs. It determines how values are embedded in systems, how authority is exercised, and how human capability is developed over time, whether in market or nonmarket settings.

Strategic architecture differs from optimization. Optimization improves isolated components. Architecture integrates interdependent systems toward the market or mission. In complex organizations, maximizing efficiency or short-term financial returns in one area often weakens performance elsewhere. Long-term success depends on the coherent alignment of capital so that judgment, trust, learning, and coordination reinforce rather than undermine one another.

When ethical capital is absent, the use of AI to support practices such as fraudulent use of images or likenesses, deceptive scams, plagiarism, and failures in data quality or algorithmic logic erodes social and organizational capital. Human capital is likewise weakened when individuals become dependent on AI for core elements of judgment, responsibility, and agency. In these conditions, capital is not optimized; it is degraded. For this reason, both AI developers and end users should begin any architectural effort with well-developed ethical capital and the capacity to demonstrate, communicate, and differentiate AI use as a responsible expression of human intent.

Organizations, societies, and individuals that protect their reputations through ethical AI use position themselves for long-term resilience and value creation. Those who misuse AI, whether deliberately or through neglect, risk marginalization and failure as technology advances and institutional expectations evolve. The intentional cultivation of ethical capital is not ancillary to innovation but a foundational exercise in capital architecture (Floridi 2019; Burrell 2016).

Multiplier Organizations

Organizations are not the sum of their assets. They are multiplier systems whose performance calculus depends on how forms of capital interact.

- Human capital provides judgment, creativity, responsibility, and agency.

- Ethical capital signals the appropriateness of intent, purpose, boundaries, and legitimacy.

- Intellectual capital expands knowledge, models, and insights.

- Structural capital embeds intention into governance, roles, and processes.

- Physical capital provides the tools for execution and experimentation.

- Financial capital allocates risk, provides liquidity, and records outcomes.

When these forms of capital are well structured and aligned, they compound human capability, institutional trust, and long-term resilience. When they are misaligned, returns concentrate in systems and controls and in short-term extraction, leaving organizations vulnerable.

Stakeholders as Sources of Capital Insight

Shareholders are often framed as the primary claimants on value or as constraints on decision-making. Within strategic capital architecture, stakeholders are better understood as sources of insight into how capital functions. Shareholders themselves are part of this stakeholder community, and their returns are strengthened, not diminished, when stakeholder insight informs how capital is built, aligned, and deployed.

Employees identify skill gaps, workflow breakdowns, and where technology supports or substitutes for human judgment. Customers and users perceive and signal trust, transparency, and legitimacy before these appear in performance metrics. Suppliers and partners expose coordination failures and structural dependencies. Communities that support organizations and care for employees' families experience the broader effects of capital deployment. Investors and funders evaluate governance quality and long-term coherence beyond near-term returns. These perspectives reveal information that no financial model can fully capture. When engaged seriously, stakeholders contribute to interpreting and aligning capital itself.

AI AND ARCHITECTURAL RISK

AI intensifies and solidifies the consequences of architectural choices. As intellectual capital, AI accelerates whatever structure it inhabits. In coherent architectures, it strengthens judgment, insight, and coordination. In poorly governed systems, it amplifies opacity, extraction, and vulnerability.

Capital budgeting in the age of AI must be treated as a strategic and moral act that determines whether technological power strengthens or undermines human capability and institutional health.

TAKEAWAYS

- AI is best understood as a form of intellectual capital that amplifies human capability rather than replacing human agency.

- The social and economic consequences of AI stem from how capital is structured, aligned, and governed, not from technological autonomy.

- Human judgment, responsibility, and action remain the source of all capital formation and effectiveness.

- Technological optimization increases leverage but also reshapes incentives, authority, and institutional risk.

- When the capital hierarchy inverts, systems begin treating tools as agents and people as inputs, undermining long-term resilience.

- AI deepens existing capital dynamics, accelerating both flourishing and extraction, depending on institutional maturity.

- Effective AI deployment requires coordinated investment across human, intellectual, structural, physical, financial, and ethical capital.

- Governance quality, not computational sophistication, determines whether AI strengthens or erodes trust, legitimacy, and productivity.

NOTES

1 Paul M. Romer, "Endogenous Technological Change," *Journal of Political Economy* 98, no. 5, pt. 2 (October 1990): S71–S102. Romer demonstrates that the stock of human capital is the primary determinant of long-run economic growth. In his model, human capital drives technological change, technological change fuels economic growth, and sustained growth, in turn, supports the further development of human capital. This framework captures the cumulative and self-reinforcing nature of technology-driven economic evolution.

2 Eric Topol, *Deep Medicine: How Artificial Intelligence Can Make Healthcare Human Again* (New York: Basic Books, 2019). Topol argues that AI can reduce physician overload by automating necessary but low value clinical and administrative tasks, including documentation, image analysis, visit coding, and routine communication. By relieving these burdens without shifting them to additional support staff, AI enables physicians to focus on the relational dimensions of care, such as listening, reassurance, interpretation, and judgment. In this way, AI has the potential to restore medicine as a healing art grounded in human connection rather than reducing it to a purely technical vocation.

3 Andre Esteva, Brett Kuprel, Roberto A. Novoa, Justin Ko, Susan M. Swetter, Helen M. Blau, and Sebastian Thrun, "Dermatologist-Level Classification of Skin Cancer with Deep Neural Networks," *Nature* 546, no. 7369 (June 28, 2017): 115–118; erratum *Nature* 546, no. 7660 (2017): 686. Esteva et al. demonstrate that well-trained convolutional neural networks can classify skin cancer from images at a level comparable to board-certified dermatologists. The study highlights the potential for scalable, low-cost diagnostic support using widely available imaging technologies, expanding access to early detection while functioning as decision support rather than a replacement for clinical judgment.

4 Daron Acemoglu and James A. Robinson, *Why Nations Fail: The Origins of Power, Prosperity, and Poverty* (New York: Crown Business, 2012); Douglass C. North, *Institutions, Institutional Change and Economic Performance* (Cambridge: Cambridge University Press, 1990); Thomas Piketty, *Capital in the Twenty-First Century*, trans. Arthur Goldhammer (Cambridge, MA: Harvard University Press, 2014); Shoshana Zuboff, *The Age of Surveillance Capitalism* (New York: Public Affairs, 2019).

WORKS CITED

Acemoglu, Daron, and Simon Johnson. 2023. *Power and Progress: Our Thousand-Year Struggle Over Technology and Prosperity.* New York: Public Affairs.

Acemoglu, Daron, and Pascual Restrepo. 2020. "Robots and Jobs: Evidence from US Labor Markets." *Journal of Political Economy* 128 (6): 2188–2244.

Acemoglu, Daron, and James A. Robinson. 2013. *Why Nations Fail: The Origins of Power, Prosperity and Poverty.* New York: Crown Currency.

Autor, David H. 2015. "Why Are There So Many Jobs? The History and Future of Workplace Automation." *Journal of Economic Perspectives* 29 (3): 3–30.

Autor, David H., David A. Mindell, and Elisabeth Reynolds. 2022. *The Work of the Future: Building Better Jobs in an Age of Intelligent Machines*. Cambridge: The MIT Press.

Baars, Bernard J. 1988. *A Cognitive Theory of Consciousness*. Cambridge: Cambridge University Press.

Bandura, Albert. 1977. *Social Learning Theory*. Englewood Cliffs, NJ: Prentice Hall.

Baumol, William J. 2013. *The Cost Disease: Why Computers Get Cheaper and Health Care Doesn't*. New Haven: Yale University Press.

Becker, Gary S. 1994. *Human Capital: A Theoretical and Empirical Analysis with Special Reference to Education* (3rd ed.). Chicago: University of Chicago Press.

Bruner, Jerome Seymour. 1990. *Acts of Meaning: Four Lectures on Mind and Culture*. Cambridge: Harvard University Press.

Brynjolfsson, Erik, and Andrew McAfee. 2016. *The Second Machine Age: Work, Progress, and Prosperity in a Time of Brilliant Technologies*. New York: W. W. Norton & Company.

Burrell, Jenna. 2016. "How the Machine 'Thinks:' Understanding Opacity in Machine Learning Algorithms." *Big Data & Society* 3 (1). Accessed January 5, 2026. https://papers.ssrn.com/sol3/papers.cfm?abstract_id=2660674

Chesney, Robert, and Danielle K. Citron. 2019. "Deep Fakes: A Looming Challenge for Privacy, Democracy and National Security." *California Law Review* 107: 1753–1819.

China. 2023, July 13. "Interim Measures for the Management of Generative Artificial Intelligence Services." *China Law Translate*. Accessed January 24, 2026. https://www.chinalawtranslate.com/en/generative-ai-interim/?utm_source=chatgpt.com

Damasio, Antonio. 2005. *Descartes' Error: Emotion, Reason, and the Human Brain*. New York: Penguin Books.

Eccles, Robert G., Ioannis Ioannou, and George Serafeim. 2014. "The Impact of Corporate Sustainability on Organizational Processes and Performance." *Management Science* 60 (11): 2835–2857.

Edmans, Alex. 2011. "Does the Stock Market Fully Value Intangibles? Employee Satisfaction and Equity Prices." *Journal of Financial Economics* 101 (3): 621–640.

Esteva, Andre, Brett Kuprel, Roberto A. Novoa, Justin Ko, Susan M. Swetter, Helen M. Blau, and Sebastin Thrun. 2017. "Dermatologist-Level Classification of Skin Cancer with Deep Neural Networks." *Nature* 546: 115–118.

Eubanks, Virginia. 2018. *Automating Inequality: How High-Tech Tools Profile, Police and Punish the Poor*. New York: St. Martin's Press.

European Union. 2024, August 2. "Artificial Intelligence Act." *artificialintelligence-act.edu*. Accessed December 28, 2025. https://artificialintelligenceact.eu/ai-act-explorer

Floridi, Luciano. 2014a, May. "Technological Unemployment, Leisure Occupation, and the Human Project." *Philosophy and Teaching* 6: 143–150.

Floridi, Luciano. 2014b. *The Fourth Revolution: How the Infosphere Is Reshaping Human Reality* (1st ed.). Oxford: Oxford University Press.

Floridi, Luciano. 2019. *The Logic of Information: A Theory of Philosophy as Conceptual Design*. Oxford, UK: Oxford University Press.

Floridi, Luciano, Josh Cowl, Monica Beltrametti, Raja Chatila, Patrice Chazerand, Virginia Dignum, Christoph Luetge, Robert Madelin, Ugo Pagallo, Francesca Rossi, Burkhard Schafer, Peggy Valcke, and Effy Vayena. 2018. "AI4People – An Ethical Framework for a Good AI Society: Opportunities, Risks, Principles, and Recommendations." *Minds and Machines* 28: 689–707.

Floridi, Luciano, and Josh Cowls. 2019. "A Unified Framework of Five Principles for AI in Society." *Harvard Data Science Review* 1 (1). doi: 10.1162/99608f92.8cd550d1

Freeman, R. Edward. 2010. *Strategic Management: A Stakeholder Approach*. Cambridge: Cambridge University Press.

Goldfarb, Avi, and Catherine Tucker. 2019. "Digital Economics." *Journal of Economic Literature* 57 (1): 3–43.

Jumper, John, Richard Evans, Alexander Pritzel, Tim Green, Michael Figurnov, Olaf Ronneberger, Kathryn Tunyasuvunakool, Russ Bates, Augustin Žídek, Anna Potapenko, Alex Bridgland, Clemens Meyer, Simon A. A. Kohl, Andrew J. Ballard, Andrew Cowie, Bernardino Romera-Paredes, Stanislav Nikolov, Rishub Jain, Jonas Adler, Trevor Back, Stig Petersen, David Reiman, Ellen Clancy, Michal Zielinski, Martin Steinegger, Michalina Pacholska, Tamas Berghammer, Sebastian Bodenstein, David Silver, Oriol Vinyals, Andrew W. Senior, Koray Kavukcuoglu, Pushmeet Kohli, and Demis Hassabis. 2021. "Highly Accurate Protein Structure Predication with AlphaFold." *Nature* 596: 583–589.

Keynes, John Maynard. 1972. *Collected Writings Vol. 9, Essays in Persuasion*. London: Macmillan.

Machlup, Fritz. 1973. *The Production and Distribution of Knowledge in the United States*. Princeton: Princeton University Press.

Marshall, Alfred. 1890. *Principles of Economics* (8th ed.). London: Macmillan and Company, Ltd.

McCormack, Jon, Toby Gifford, Patrick Hutchings, Jon McCormack, Toby Gifford, Patrick Hutchings, Maria Teresa Llano Rodriguez, Matthew Yee-King, and Mark d'Inverno. 2019. "In a Silent Way: Communication Between AI and Human Musicians Beyond Sound." *Proceedings of the 2019 CHI Conference on Human Factors in Computing Science*, 1–11.

Modigliani, Franco, and Merton H. Miller. 1958. "The Cost of Capital, Corporation Finance and the Theory of Investment." *The American Economic Review* 48 (3): 261–297.

North, Douglass C. 1990. *Institutions, Institutional Change and Economic Performance*. Cambridge: Cambridge University Press.

Parasuraman, Raja, and Victor Riley. 1997. "Humans and Automation: Use, Misuse, Disuse, Abuse." *Human Factors* 39 (2): 230–253.

Piketty, Thomas. 2014. *Capital in the Twenty-First Century*. Translated by Arthur Goldhammer. Cambridge: Belknap Press.

Polanyi, Michael. 2019. *The Tacit Dimension*. Chicago: The University of Chicago Press.

Porter, Michael E., and Mark R. Kramer. 2011. "Creating Shared Value." *Harvard Business Review* 89 (1–2): 62–77.

Romer, Paul M. 1990. "Endogenous Technological Change." *Journal of Political Economy* 98 (5, Part 2): S71–S102.

Roos, Johan, Goran Roos, Leif Edvinsson, and Nicola Dragonetti. 1997. *Intellectual Capital: Navigating in the New Business Landscape.* London: Palgrave Macmillan.

Russell, Stuart, and Peter Norvig. 2021. *Artificial Intelligence: A Modern Approach* (4th ed.). Hoboken, NJ: Pearson.

Sahni, Nikhil R., George Stein, Rodney Zemmel, and David Cutler. 2024. "The Potential Impact of Artificial Intelligence on Health Care Spending." In *The Economics of Artificial Intelligence: Health Care Challenges*, edited by Ajay Agrawal, Joshua Gans, Avi Goldfarb, and Catherine E. Tucker, 49–86. Chicago: University of Chicago Press.

Schultz, Theodore W. 1961. "Investment in Human Capital." *The American Economic Review* 51 (1): 1–17.

Schumpeter, Joseph A. 1942. *Capitalism, Socialism, and Democracy.* New York: Harper & Brothers.

Smith, Adam. 1977. *An Inquiry into the Nature and Causes of the Wealth of Nations.* Reprint. Chicago: University of Chicago Press.

Solow, Robert M. 1956. "A Contribution to the Theory of Economic Growth." *Quarterly Journal of Economics* 70 (1): 65–94.

Stewart, Thomas A. 1997. *Intellectual Capital: The New Wealth of Organizations.* New York: Currency.

Topol, Eric. 2019. *Deep Medicine: How Artificial Intelligence Can Make Healthcare Human Again.* New York: Basic Books.

Zuboff, Shoshana. 1989. *In the Age of the Smart Machine: The Future of Work.* New York: Basic Books.

Zuboff, Shoshana. 2019. *The Age of Surveillance Capitalism: The Fight for a Human Future at the New Frontier of Power.* New York: Public Affairs.

CHAPTER 3

Human Capital in the Age of AI

HUMAN CAPITAL AS THE LIVING CORE OF THE CAPITAL SYSTEM

Human capital is the only form of capital that resides within humans and supports agency and action. It is the tacit form of capital that uniquely enables humans to access and use all other forms of capital. Other forms of capital amplify, transmit, or embed human intention. To fully appreciate the architecture of capital, it is essential to broaden the discussion of human capital to include its unique nature, development, and attributes.

Humans develop their human capital, pool it with others, and leverage it, but timing, developmental cycles, and experiences mediate this unique form of capital. Human capital development, deployment, and decay create a unique and highly differentiated arc of deepening and alignment, shaped by society, family, peers, teachers, institutions, and individual talents and experiences.

Unlike financial or physical capital, human capital cannot be accumulated quickly or deployed mechanically. It is formed through lived experience, guided practice, social learning, and moral development. Skills, habits, judgment, and character develop gradually and unevenly over a lifetime. These capacities mature through relationships and responsibility, not merely from exposure to information. When development is bypassed or compressed, the potential for future performance may erode quietly.

DOI: 10.1201/9781003744061-3

Artificial intelligence (AI) interacts with human capital asymmetrically. It can expand access to information, accelerate feedback, and support learning when embedded appropriately. It can also displace effort, weaken attention, and reduce opportunities for judgment when introduced without regard to developmental readiness. Because AI operates at scale and speed, these effects compound quickly. The result is not neutral. It shapes how people learn to reason, decide, and act.

For this reason, human capital is the binding constraint in AI-enabled systems. Organizations may expand technical capacity, automate workflows, and optimize outputs, but they cannot bypass the time-consuming work of developing capable people who guide value-creating activities. When human development is neglected, capital systems become vulnerable and dependent, often proving difficult to govern. When human formation is prioritized, AI becomes a powerful extension of human capability.

Architectural impatience in designing and deploying capital systems often leads organizational and societal leaders astray. AI is not a magic elixir that accelerates human capital formation; it can scaffold and support development. Human capital cannot be compressed without cost. When policymakers, educational institutions, or other social actors attempt to accelerate human development beyond its natural pace, they risk undermining the uniquely human processes of developing judgment, responsibility, and experience, on which social and organizational success ultimately depends (Piaget 2005; Kohlberg 1981; Marzano and Kendall 2006).

HUMAN AGENCY AND DEVELOPMENT

Human agency is not an abstract capacity that appears fully formed. It involves more than the ability to choose. It also requires perception, maturation, self-regulation, and the capacity to anticipate consequences. These abilities develop over time and are shaped by social environments, expectations, and feedback.

Economic and psychological research consistently shows that agency is cultivated through effort and accountability rather than passive exposure to information. Individuals learn to exercise judgment by confronting uncertainty, making mistakes, and integrating feedback. Habits of attention, perseverance, and moral reasoning develop through repeated engagement with real problems and consequences, not through simulation alone. Human capital develops through participation in meaningful activity that demands discernment and growth in responsibility.

AI alters the conditions under which agency develops. When AI supports learning, reflection, and feedback, it can strengthen agency by expanding understanding and easing cognitive and procedural burdens. When AI substitutes for effort, decision-making, or responsibility, it weakens agency by removing opportunities to develop sound judgment. The difference lies not in the sophistication of the technology but in how it is positioned within developmental processes.

Agency is also relational. People learn to make decisions by observing others. Social learning plays a central role in shaping norms, expectations, and standards of behavior (Bandura 1977). Over time, these social signals influence how individuals understand responsibility and autonomy. AI can contribute to human development and alignment with social signals through well-designed scaffolding. It can also diminish human capital when used poorly, bypassing essential developmental events and social signals.

Because human agency develops slowly and unevenly, timing matters. Introducing AI into contexts where judgment is still forming carries different consequences than introducing it into settings where judgment is already mature.

For this reason, human agency must be treated as a developmental capacity rather than an assumed constant. AI-enabled systems that fail to account for this reality may undermine people's long-term capacity to reason, decide, and act independently. Systems that respect the developmental nature of agency create the conditions for AI to support human flourishing.

FAMILY AS THE FIRST DEVELOPER OF HUMAN CAPITAL

Human capital formation begins long before individuals enter formal education or the workplace. The family is the first developmental environment where attention, responsibility, language, and trust are formed. It is within families that early habits of learning, self-regulation, and moral orientation take shape. These early experiences establish developmental pathways that later investments in education, work, and institutions either reinforce or struggle to repair.

Economic research on human capital formation shows that early capabilities strongly shape later outcomes. Flavio Cunha and James Heckman (2007) demonstrate that skills are built cumulatively over time, with early cognitive and non-cognitive development increasing the value of later investments. These dynamic building blocks of sequential development underscore that early formation cannot be easily substituted or, when malformed, reversed later. When foundational capabilities are weak, subsequent interventions face diminishing returns and higher costs (Heckman 2006).[1]

Research on childhood inequality supports this conclusion. Greg Duncan and Katherine Magnuson (2011) show that disparities in early family conditions are strongly linked to long-term differences in educational attainment, health, and economic mobility. While schools and social programs can mitigate some effects, they cannot fully compensate for early deficits in stability, attention, and support. Human capital development is path-dependent and cumulative rather than modular or easily accelerated.

Developmental science further shows that early environments shape the biological and cognitive systems that underlie later learning and judgment. Jack Shonkoff et al. (2012) demonstrate that prolonged exposure to stress, instability, and neglect in early childhood can disrupt executive function, emotional regulation, and learning capacity through physiological pathways. These effects persist over time and limit the effectiveness of subsequent remediation efforts, underscoring the importance of early relational stability for healthy human capital development.

These early differences in human capital formation also shape how individuals participate in regional and organizational economies later in life. Enrico Moretti (2013) highlights that concentrations of skilled human capital generate spillover effects that raise productivity, wages, and innovation across communities. These cumulative effects amplify early advantages and make later remediation more difficult, underscoring the importance of human capital formation within families.

Families shape how agency is exercised by modeling judgment, effort, and accountability. Children learn not only what to think but also how to think, act, and respond through observation, imitation, and guided participation (Bandura 1977; Bruner 1990).

Increasingly, AI and AI-enabled technologies shape family life through media, communication tools, educational platforms, and household technologies. These systems influence attention, interaction, and expectations in subtle but persistent ways. When AI supports parental guidance, shared learning, and age-appropriate exploration, it can complement family-based development. When it substitutes for supervision, conversation, or responsibility, it can displace the relational processes through which judgment and self-control develop.

Timing and mediation matter. Early exposure to automated recommendations, predictive systems, or continuous stimulation can shape preferences and habits before critical capacities are formed. Because family life is the first environment in which norms are learned, the uncritical introduction of AI can unintentionally reinforce dependence rather than capability. Conversely, intentional use that reinforces effort, patience, and reflection can strengthen early development rather than undermine it. AI use needs clear guidelines and family supervision during the formative years.

Family-based formation lays the earliest foundations of human capital, but it does not complete the work of development. As children move beyond the household, educational institutions assume responsibility for extending and stabilizing the habits of attention, effort, and judgment first shaped within families. Effective education functions as a partnership rather than a substitute. Schools inherit developmental pathways formed at home and translate them into shared standards of knowledge, responsibility, and social participation. Where the family and education align, human capital compounds over time. Where the two drift apart, educational systems face limits that no curriculum, technology, or remediation can fully overcome.

STAGED HUMAN CAPITAL FORMATION: FORMAL EDUCATION

Educational institutions serve as the primary bridge between family-based formation and participation in broader social and economic systems. Their central role is not the transmission of information but the staged development of human capability. Education transforms early dispositions toward attention, effort, and trust into structured opportunities for learning, judgment, and action. When this developmental role is misunderstood, schooling risks prioritizing credentials and throughput over the formation of sustainable, thriving humans with well-developed human capital.

Learning unfolds in staged sequences shaped by cognitive and moral readiness and developmental timing (Kohlberg 1981; Piaget 2005). Foundational skills in literacy, numeracy, and self-regulation enable later abstraction, reasoning, and problem-solving. Research consistently shows that effective education builds capability cumulatively rather than instantaneously. Teacher quality, expectations, and feedback matter more than curriculum novelty or technological intensity in shaping long-term outcomes (Hanushek and Rivkin 2012). Instruction aligned with developmental readiness strengthens persistence, confidence, and skill transfer. Instruction that advances too quickly often produces surface performance without foundational understanding.

Educational opportunity is also shaped by place and context. Socioeconomic inequality influences the resources, stability, and cognitive load students bring to classrooms. Sean Reardon (2011) shows that disparities in family income and neighborhood conditions translate into widening achievement gaps that schools alone cannot overcome. Educational institutions operate within constraints that affect developmental outcomes. While schooling can mitigate inequality, it cannot fully compensate for upstream differences in opportunity. Age- and development-specific AI tools, in which algorithms and data are trained for specific groups, are a luxury for many schools.

As AI is increasingly used in educational settings through tutoring systems, assessment tools, content platforms, creativity tools, instructional support, and administrative support, it is critical that teachers and parents actively participate in AI development and implementation. When embedded appropriately, AI can support feedback, pacing, and diagnostic insight. When positioned as a substitute for instruction or judgment, it risks compressing developmental sequences and weakening foundational skills. The educational value of AI depends not on expansive sophistication but on whether it supports staged learning and preserves the relational structure of teaching.

Education also shapes non-cognitive development alongside academic skills by cultivating higher-order capacities that govern how knowledge is used. Motivation, higher-order skills, self-regulation, and metacognitive awareness develop through sustained interaction with capable adults, clear expectations, and structured opportunities for reflection. Metacognition is the ability to monitor, evaluate, and adapt one's own thinking and learning strategies. Higher-order skills involve analysis, judgment, and transfer across contexts (Marzano and Kendall 2006).

These advanced capacities shape how learners respond to challenges, ambiguity, and uncertainty in social and professional settings. AI can indirectly support these processes by reducing the administrative burden of learning and enabling more focused human engagement. It cannot replace the formative role of educators, peers, and parents in cultivating judgment and responsibility. The effective development of these higher-order cognitive functions and abilities also shapes how effectively an individual uses AI.

Education should be understood as a developmental system rather than a production process. Its success depends on aligning instruction, assessment, and technology use with the stages of human capability development. AI strengthens education when it respects this sequence and supports human instruction.

SIDEBAR 3.1   EDUCATIONAL STAGING, EARLY RETURNS, AND AI

Research on the economics of education shows that the highest social and economic returns occur in the early stages of learning:

- Harry Patrinos and George Psacharopoulos (2004) demonstrate that primary education yields stronger and more consistent returns on human capital than later educational investments, particularly when foundational skills are unevenly developed.
- Early educational investment lays the foundation for later learning, productivity, and adaptability throughout an individual's life.
- When early education or family-based human capital formation is weak and not promptly addressed, later investments in secondary or higher education yield diminishing returns and may impair workplace performance.
- Education should be treated as a human capital investment, with effectiveness shaped as much by developmental timing as by investment intensity.

AI as pedagogical support:

- Research on intelligent tutoring systems shows that AI can support learning when it scaffolds practice, provides feedback, and adjusts pacing.
- Kurt VanLehn (2011) shows that AI- and technology-driven systems are effective at reinforcing skills and supporting comprehension, particularly when they complement human instruction.
- Intelligent tutoring systems do not replace mentored judgment, motivation, or responsibility in learners.
- AI and technology's effectiveness depends on being embedded within instructional relationships rather than on being positioned as autonomous authorities.
- AI strengthens education when it extends teachers' instructional reach without displacing their formative role.

COMMUNITIES AND CULTURAL TRADITIONS AS HUMAN AND ETHICAL CAPITAL

Human capital formation does not end with family or formal education. Beyond these foundational institutions, individuals are shaped by deeper orientations of trust, meaning, and purpose that guide judgment when rules are incomplete and outcomes uncertain. These orientations are often described as faith traditions, though not all take the form of organized religion. In practice, every individual operates within some framework of ultimate concern, whether grounded in religious belief, secular ideology, professional identity, nationalism, progress, market rationality, or personal autonomy. These frameworks function as lived faiths insofar as they organize loyalty, justify sacrifice, and anchor responsibility across time and uncertainty.

Communities form around these shared commitments and transmit them through narratives, rituals, norms, and expectations that shape conscience and behavior. Sociological and philosophical research consistently shows that such meaning-making systems are unavoidable features of human social life rather than optional beliefs held by a few. As Paul Tillich argued, faith is defined not by its object but by its function as an ultimate concern that orders life and action (Tillich 1958). Whether explicit or implicit, these faith traditions shape how individuals understand obligation, authority, dignity, and the proper use of power. In this sense, moral and cultural communities serve as formative infrastructure for human and ethical capital, influencing how AI and other technologies are interpreted, trusted, resisted, or embraced.

Faith communities, social institutions, shared communities of interest, and cultural traditions contribute to human capital by cultivating conscience and ethical formation. They shape how individuals interpret choice, consequences, obligations, authority, sacrifice, and accountability in everyday life. These interpretations inform routine decisions about honesty, effort, cooperation, and care for others and persist across professional, civic, and organizational contexts. Over time, they form habits of judgment that cannot be easily replicated through formal training or technical instruction alone. These faith-shaped structures serve as building blocks for ethical or unethical uses of AI and technology.

From a capital perspective, these traditions foster the formation of ethical capital and individual ethical capacity. They develop internal constraints that reduce the need for external enforcement. Institutional economics has long recognized that shared moral norms and social trust lower transaction costs, stabilize expectations, and enable cooperation in complex systems (North 1990; Fukuyama 1995). Where ethical formation is strong, organizations and societies rely less on surveillance, rigid controls, and punitive mechanisms. Where it is weak, formal systems compensate, often at high cost and with limited effectiveness.

Social science research further supports the role of moral and cultural traditions in sustaining institutional performance. Communities with dense networks of trust, shared norms, and civic engagement exhibit greater institutional resilience and coordination capacity (Putnam 2001). These forms of social trust are not spontaneous outcomes of markets or technologies. They are cultivated over time through shared practices, moral commitments, and communal responsibility.

AI interacts with moral and cultural formation indirectly but powerfully. By mediating information, shaping attention, and influencing norms at scale, AI systems participate in environments that reinforce or erode ethical habits. When AI is introduced without regard for moral formation, it can normalize trends, diffuse responsibility, and obscure accountability. When integrated into communities and institutions that already cultivate ethical judgment, AI can extend coordination and insight without displacing moral agency.

It is essential to distinguish ethical formation from ethical governance. Ethical capacity develops within individuals through lived experience, reflection, and moral development, not solely through regulatory systems. Governance frameworks, institutional rules, and formal oversight mechanisms rely on ethical capital, but they cannot generate it. They function effectively only when supported by people whose judgment, restraint, and sense of responsibility are already well formed. Without this foundation, ethical rules lose their force. Compliance becomes procedural rather than principled, and systems increasingly depend on surveillance, enforcement, and control to achieve minimal conformity (North 1990).

Faith, moral, communal, and cultural traditions serve as formative infrastructure for human and ethical capital. They shape the internal capacities that enable people to exercise judgment responsibly in environments marked by uncertainty, power, and technological scale. As AI expands the reach and speed of informing choice, the importance of these formative traditions increases rather than diminishes.

SOCIAL LEARNING AND AI-MEDIATED FORMATION

Social learning operates continuously, shaping how judgment, effort, and responsibility are exercised over time (Bandura 1977). In traditional settings, social learning unfolded through face-to-face interaction within bounded communities. Norms were transmitted through role models, peer behavior, mentorship, and shared institutional practices. These processes reinforced accountability because behavior was visible, relationships were stable, and consequences were local. Social learning supported the gradual development of trust, self-regulation, and moral judgment alongside technical skills.

AI fundamentally alters this environment by mediating social learning at scale. Digital platforms and recommendation systems curate exposure to behaviors, opinions, and values across vast networks. These systems shape attention by amplifying certain signals and suppressing others, effectively influencing what is seen, imitated, and normalized. As a result, social learning is no longer constrained by proximity or institutional boundaries but increasingly governed by algorithmic selection, data curation, and trending behavior.

Earlier forms of mass media, such as television, radio, and the early Internet, operated primarily through broad dissemination and relatively passive consumption. While they influenced norms, exposure was more uniform and selective attention rested mainly with the audience. AI-driven systems differ by continuously adapting content to individual behavior, integrating values, norms, and behavioral cues into personalized streams. This nuanced and persistent mediation embeds norm formation within everyday interaction rather than in discrete acts of consumption.

AI recommendation systems are typically optimized for engagement rather than formation. Content that elicits strong emotional responses, is novel, or offers rapid feedback is preferentially amplified by algorithmic ranking systems designed to maximize attention and time on the platform (Zuboff 2019; Gillespie 2018). While this design can spread creativity, generosity, and civic participation, it can also accelerate polarization, misinformation, and performative behavior (Bakshy, Messing, and Adamic 2015; Bail et al. 2018). The same mechanisms that elevate constructive norms can normalize short-termism, outrage, and moral disengagement when engagement is rewarded independently of truth or responsibility (Sunstein 2017). AI intensifies these tendencies by increasing speed, scale, and repetition, amplifying whatever users attend to most consistently (Bandura 1977; Gillespie 2018).

From a human capital perspective, this mediated environment reshapes the development of judgment and self-regulation. Repeated exposure to AI reinforces signals, shaping expectations about success, identity, and social reward. When systems reward immediacy, visibility, and reactivity rather than reflection and responsibility, they encourage surface engagement rather than depth. These incentives affect motivation, attention, and ethical reasoning, all of which are core components of human capital formation.

Because AI systems operate through probabilistic ranking and feedback loops, they implicitly embed judgments about which behaviors to amplify. Although their technical logic may be neutral in intent, their effects are not. By shaping visibility and imitation, AI systems participate directly in norm formation. AI resides at the intersection of exposure to intellectual capital and human capital formation, shaping not only what people know but also how they learn to value, judge, and act (Gillespie 2018). Unlike books or other forms of relatively static media, which can be curated, paced, and contextualized through human judgment, AI-generated content and guidance adapt continuously, often outpacing the deliberative processes through which meaning and responsibility are traditionally formed.

Explicit forms of ethical capital, shaped within families, educational institutions, social institutions, and work environments, play a decisive role in moderating AI's effects on human ethical capacity. Platforms and institutions that prioritize transparency, accountability, and human dignity can design systems that elevate constructive norms and support civic responsibility. Educational, familial, and workplace environments reinforce this alignment by cultivating critical reflection, media literacy, and moral reasoning that anchor judgment amid AI influence. Where such ethical capital is absent or implicit, social learning becomes detached from accountability, and human capital formation drifts toward fragmentation.

Social learning remains a powerful engine of human development. AI cannot replace this process, but it can amplify it. Whether that amplification strengthens judgment and character or accelerates erosion depends on how intellectual capital is governed, how ethical capital deployment is embedded in supportive social institutions, and how it aligns with human capital formation. These outcomes are not technological accidents. They are consequences of capital architecture and collective choice.

ORGANIZATIONAL STRUCTURAL ARCHITECTURE, AI, AND HUMANS

An organization's structural capital shapes how human capital is deployed, amplified, or constrained. While families, schools, and moral traditions shape human capability, organizations are where that capability is tested under conditions of complexity, coordination, and consequence. Organizational structural capital encompasses the allocation of decision rights, the design of workflows, the distribution of authority, and the mechanisms for maintaining accountability. These elements shape how judgment is exercised and whether human capital development and deployment mature or deteriorate over time.

Successful organizations recognize that human capital is not uniform. Judgment develops unevenly, experience accumulates at different rates, and ethical capacity varies across roles and contexts. Organizational structures should align responsibility with capability, particularly in knowledge-intensive and professional environments where discretion and expertise cannot be fully standardized (Quinn, Anderson, and Finkelstein 1996). When authority is delegated to individuals with well-formed judgment, organizations benefit from adaptability, initiative, and learning. When decision-making is overly centralized or automated beyond human developmental capacity, organizations constrain the development of judgment, weaken succession pathways, and ultimately limit the long-term creation of human capital.

Architectural failures often emerge when organizational architects blur the boundaries between forms of capital and pursue substitution rather than alignment. AI, as intellectual capital and a facilitator of structural capital, is frequently deployed as a neutral efficiency tool, even though it reshapes authority, judgment, and learning pathways. An overabundance of intellectual or structural capital cannot substitute for human capital, which remains the engine of value creation.

Over time, this substitution can erode agency, weaken institutional memory, and undermine trust. Effective organizational architecture requires maintaining clear lanes for each form of capital and deliberately crafting the right level and balance of human capital so that the organization can thrive, renew itself, and sustain value over time.

Societies face a parallel challenge in the public square. Just as organizations cannot substitute intellectual or structural capital for human judgment, policymakers and institutional support systems cannot centrally engineer the quantity or quality of human capital needed to sustain economic vitality and human flourishing. Social systems depend on long-term processes of formation that unfold across families, schools, communities, and workplaces. When public policy treats human capital as a variable to be optimized rather than a capacity to be cultivated over time, it risks undermining the very foundations of social coordination, trust, and prosperity.

Effective capital architecture integrates AI in ways that respect human limits and developmental pathways. Decision-support systems are effective only when paired with clear role definitions, explicit escalation pathways, and structured opportunities for reflection. Where judgment is still forming, AI should be used to scaffold human growth. Where judgment is maturing, particularly among emerging leaders, AI aligned with structural and ethical capital standards can extend reach and consistency without displacing accountability.

Organizations adapt more quickly than formal institutions and often serve as social testing grounds for new technological arrangements. The success or failure of AI within organizations signals broader societal consequences early on. Viewing organizational architecture as the deployment environment for human capital clarifies why some AI-enabled systems strengthen judgment and trust while others accelerate fragmentation and dependence. Organizations are society's AI Petri dishes.

This architectural perspective lays the groundwork for examining how formal institutions, markets, and governance structures respond when organizational experimentation outpaces human formation. The limits observed within organizations reveal the constraints that must be addressed as AI reshapes systems at larger scales.

SIDEBAR 3.2   AI AND HUMAN CAPITAL RISKS

- Over-automation compresses developmental learning cycles, reducing opportunities to develop judgment, effort, and responsibility over time.
- Systems that reward output without understanding long-term human capital development undermine succession, producing short-term performance at the expense of long-term human capability.
- When responsibility shifts from people to systems, accountability becomes diffuse, eroding agency and moral ownership of decisions.
- Cognitive flattening occurs when higher-order thinking is replaced by procedural efficiency, leaving individuals skilled in execution but weak in judgment and in transferring knowledge and skills to new situations.

- AI amplifies existing strengths or weaknesses in human capital, depending on whether it is embedded in a formative or a substitutive architecture.
- Ethical and organizational architecture determines whether AI deepens human judgment and trust or accelerates dependence and the erosion of human capital.

TABLE 3.1   The Role of AI in Human Capital Development

Developmental Capacity	Primary Human Function	Appropriate Role of AI	Risk if Misapplied
Foundational cognition	Understanding, recall	Practice, feedback	Overreliance on prompting
Skill acquisition	Application, execution	Simulation, scaffolding	Skill atrophy
Metacognition	Self-regulation, knowledge/skill transfer	Reflection support	Cognitive flattening
Moral reasoning	Judgment, responsibility	Transparency support	Accountability diffusion
Social intelligence	Trust, cooperation	Coordination aid	Relational breakdown

Table 3.1 provides a concise reference for understanding AI's role in human capital development across the developmental life cycle. It highlights how AI can support learning, judgment, and coordination at different stages and clarifies the risks that arise when technological support is misaligned with developmental capacity.

HUMAN CAPITAL AND AI: A DEVELOPMENTAL CODA

Developmental research shows that individuals move from concrete understanding toward abstraction, from externally guided behavior toward internalized responsibility, and from rule-following toward principled judgment (Piaget 2005; Kohlberg 1981). AI can support these processes, but cannot replace them. When developmental sequencing is ignored or accelerated prematurely, it often masks long-term losses in adaptability, responsibility, and judgment.

Learning is iterative rather than sequential. Understanding emerges through cycles of action, feedback, effort, and reflection. Experiential learning depends on engagement with real problems and opportunities for revision (Kolb 1983). Research on learning and memory shows that effortful practice, active retrieval, and spaced repetition strengthen long-term retention and transfer, even when they slow initial performance (Bjork and Bjork 2011). Motivation also plays a central role. Learning environments that support autonomy, competence, and purpose foster deeper engagement than those optimized solely for speed or efficiency (Ryan and Deci 2000). AI can assist by providing feedback, simulation, and practice, but when it removes effort entirely or substitutes for reflection, it weakens the very capacities it is meant to support.

Educational research consistently distinguishes between lower-order cognitive tasks and higher-order functions such as analysis, evaluation, and self-regulation (Anderson et al. 2001; Marzano and Kendall 2006). AI systems excel at retrieval, pattern recognition, and procedural execution. However, they lack self-regulation, moral reasoning, and a sense of responsibility. With appropriate structuring, AI can support human development through guided exploration that illustrates the consequences of the proper and improper use of these very human higher-order attributes.

Human intelligence is plural, not singular. People demonstrate capability through multiple forms of intelligence, including analytical, creative, social, physical, practical, and moral dimensions (Gardner 1999, 2011). These capacities are embodied, relational, and context-dependent. AI interacts unevenly with these plural forms of intelligence, amplifying certain analytical and procedural functions. Effective human capital development requires environments that recognize and support this diversity of capabilities.

AI can enhance human capital only when it aligns with developmental realities. It can scaffold learning, extend reach, offer opportunities for exploration, and improve coordination, but it cannot accelerate development beyond human limits. These constraints shape how AI should be deployed within organizations, governed by institutions, and evaluated by societies.

SIDEBAR 3.3   FOUNDATIONS OF HUMAN CAPITAL

- Human capital develops sequentially across cognitive, moral, and social dimensions (Piaget 2005; Kohlberg 1981).
- Judgment and responsibility emerge through experience and consequences, not from instruction alone.
- Learning is strengthened by effort, feedback, and reflection rather than by frictionless optimization (Bjork and Bjork 2011).
- Motivation, autonomy, and purpose are central to sustained learning and capability development (Ryan and Deci 2000).
- AI interacts differently at each stage of development and should not bypass formative processes.

TAKEAWAYS

- Human capital remains the primary source of judgment, agency, and value creation across all technological and capital systems.

- Human capital is developed, not merely deployed. Family, education, work, and social institutions shape the conditions in which judgment, responsibility, and adaptability emerge.

- AI alters the environments of formation rather than replacing formative processes. It mediates attention, learning, feedback, and social modeling at scale, intensifying both positive and negative developmental pathways.

- Early human capital formation compounds over time. Foundational investments in cognition, self-regulation, and ethical capacity enhance the productivity of later education, training, and social and organizational participation.

- Education functions as capital formation rather than throughput. AI strengthens learning when it scaffolds effort, retrieval, exploration, discovery, reflection, and feedback, but weakens formation when it substitutes for judgment or discipline.

- Human agency weakens when responsibility is delegated to systems.

- Ethical capacity develops in people, not in systems. Governance frameworks depend on ethical capital but cannot replace well-formed individuals.

- Organizations should align authority with developmental capability. AI-enabled organizational architecture succeeds when responsibility, discretion, and accountability reflect human maturity and role-specific judgment.

- Capital substitution, rather than purposeful capital architecture, erodes resilience. Excess intellectual or structural capital cannot replace human capital.

NOTE

1 Flavio Cunha and James Heckman, "The Technology of Skill Formation," *American Economic Review* 97, no. 2 (2007): 31–47. The authors develop a life-cycle model showing that early investments in cognitive and noncognitive skills compound over time by increasing the productivity of later investments, underscoring the cumulative nature of human capital formation.

WORKS CITED

Anderson, Lorin, David Krathwohl, Peter Airasian, Kathleen Cruikshank, Richard Mayer, Paul Pintrich, James Raths, and Merlin Wittrock. 2001. *Taxonomy for Learning, Teaching, and Assessing: A Revision of Bloom's Taxonomy of Educational Objectives*. Boston: Pearson.

Bail, Christopher A., Lisa P. Argyle, Taylor W. Brown, John P. Bumpus, Haohan Chen, M.B. Fallin Hunzaker, Jaemin Lee, Marcus Mann, Friedolin Merhout, and Alexander Volfovsky. 2018. "Exposure to Opposing Views on Social Media Can Increase Political Polarization." *Proceedings of the National Academy of Sciences of the United States of America* 115 (37): 9216–9221.

Bakshy, Eytan, Solomon Messing, and Lada A. Adamic. 2015. "Exposure to Ideologically Diverse News and Opinion on Facebook." *Science* 348 (6239): 1130–1132.

Bandura, Albert. 1977. *Social Learning Theory*. Englewood Cliffs, NJ: Prentice Hall.

Bjork, E., and R. Bjork. 2011. "Making Things Harder on Yourself, but in a Good Way: Creating Desirable Difficulties to Enhance Learning." In *Psychology and the Real World: Essays Illustrating Fundamental Contributions to Society*, edited by M.A. Gernsbacher, R. W. Pew, L. M. Hough and J. R. Pomerantz, 56–64. Worth Publishers.

Bruner, Jerome Seymour. 1990. *Acts of Meaning: Four Lectures on Mind and Culture*. Cambridge: Harvard University Press.

Cunha, Flavio, and James Heckman. 2007. "The Technology of Skill Formation." *American Economic Review* 97 (2): 31–47.

Duncan, Greg J., and Katherine Magnuson. 2011. "The Nature and Impact of Early Achievement Skills, Attention Skills, and Behavior Problems." In *Whither Opportunity?: Rising Inequality, Schools, and Children's Life Chances*, edited by Greg J. Duncan and Richard J. Murnane, 47–69. New York: Russell Sage.

Fukuyama, Francis. 1995. *Trust: The Social Virtues and the Creation of Prosperity*. New York: Free Press.

Gardner, Howard. 1999. *Intelligence Reframes: Multiple Intelligences for the 21st Century*. New York: Basic Books.

Gardner, Howard. 2011. *Frames of Mind: The Theory of Multiple Intelligences*. New York: Basic Books.

Gillespie, Tarleton. 2018. *Custodians of the Internet: Platforms, Content Moderation, and the Hidden Decisions That Shape Social Media*. New Haven: Yale University Press.

Hanushek, Eric A., and Steven G. Rivkin. 2012. "The Distribution of Teacher Quality and Implications for Policy." *Annual Review of Economics* 4 (1): 131–157.

Heckman, James. 2006. "Skill Formation and the Economics of Investing in Disadvantaged Children." *Science* 312 (5782): 1900–1902.

Kohlberg, Lawrence. 1981. *The Philosophy of Moral Development: Moral Stages and the Idea of Justice*, Vol. 1. Essays on Moral Development. San Francisco, CA: Harper & Row.

Kolb, David A. 1983. *Experiential Learning: Experience as the Source of Learning and Development.* Englewood Cliffs: Prentice Hall.

Marzano, Robert J., and John S. Kendall. 2006. *The New Taxonomy of Educational Objectives* (2nd ed.). Thousand Oaks, CA: Corwin.

Moretti, Enrico. 2013. *The New Geography of Jobs.* Boston, MA: Harper Business.

North, Douglass C. 1990. *Institutions, Institutional Change and Economic Performance.* Cambridge, UK: Cambridge University Press.

Patrinos, Harry Anthony, and George Psacharopoulos. 2004. "Returns to Investment in Education: A Further Update." *Education Economics* 12 (2): 111–134.

Piaget, Jean. 2005. *The Psychology of Intelligence.* New York: Routledge.

Putnam, Robert D. 2001. *Bowling Alone: The Collapse and Revival of American Community.* New York: Touchstone Books.

Quinn, James Brian, Philip W. Anderson, and Sydney Finkelstein. 1996. "Managing Professional Intellect: Making the Most of the Best." *Harvard Business Review* 74 (2), 71–80.

Reardon, Sean F. 2011. "The Widening Academic Achievement Gap between the Rich and the Poor." *Community Investments* 24 (2): 19–39.

Ryan, Richard M., and Edward L. Deci. 2000. "Intrinsic and Extrinsic Motivations: Classic Definitions and New Directions." *Contemporary Educational Psychology* 25 (1): 54–67.

Shonkoff, Jack P., Andrew S. Garner, Benjamin S. Siegel, Mary I. Dobbins, Marian F. Earls, Andrew S. Garner, Laura McGuinn, John Pascoe, David L. Wood, Pamela C. High, Elaine Donoghue, Jill J. Fussell, Mary Margaret Gleason, Paula K. Jaudes, Veronnie F. Jones, David M. Rubin, Elaine E. Schulte, Michelle M. Macias, Carolyn Bridgemohan, Jill Fussell, Edward Goldson, Laura J. McGuinn, Carol Weitzman, and Lynn Mowbray Wegner. 2012. "The Lifelong Effects of Early Childhood Adversity and Toxic Stress." *Pediatrics* 129 (1): e232–e246.

Sunstein, Cass R. 2017. *#Republic: Divided Democracy in the Age of Social Media.* Princeton, NJ: Princeton University Press.

Tillich, Paul. 1958. *Dynamics of Faith.* New York: HarperCollins.

VanLehn, Kurt. 2011. "The Relative Effectiveness of Human Tutoring, Intelligent Tutoring Systems and Other Tutoring Systems." *Educational Psychologist* 46 (4): 197–221.

Zuboff, Shoshana. 2019. *The Age of Surveillance Capitalism: The Fight for a Human Future at the New Frontier of Power.* New York: Public Affairs.

CHAPTER 4

Ethical Capital

AI Governance

ETHICAL CAPITAL AND AI

Artificial intelligence (AI) is often hyped as the next breakthrough tool that will solve vexing social and economic problems and spark the next economic revolution. Others prophesy doom and the economic collapse of the working and middle classes. These claims echo a late eighteenth-century treatise by Thomas Malthus (2018), which predicted that a dystopian future would result from food supply growing arithmetically and population growing exponentially, diminishing life. In hindsight, Malthus failed to account for the role of capital in leveraging human and agricultural capital to expand the food supply and keep pace with human population growth. A second oversight was the inability to envision ethical considerations that would refocus global food production and even capitalism, leading to an uneven but continuous upward trend.

In response to Malthus' glum portrait, the mid-eighteenth-century writer Charles Dickens (2008) aimed at the Malthusian logic embedded in the Victorian Poor Laws and the social gloom of capitalism with his novel 'A Christmas Carol.' Dickens also aimed at the ethics of the prevailing capitalist system. The book tapped a social nerve, and while it created a moral vision for the use of money, property, and human flourishing in its day, it was also an imaginative portrait of ethical capital and human ethical capacity, as Scrooge is transformed.

DOI: 10.1201/9781003744061-4

As Dickens so clearly highlighted, capital has political and commercial power, and that power shapes how humans live, work, and flourish. When authority corrupts social policy, commercial activity, and human development, social repulsion and withdrawal unfold, much like the Malthus–Dickens dialogue. This withdrawal rarely occurs all at once. It unfolds gradually through disengagement and loss of confidence. What prevents this dissolution, as Scrooged learned, is an ethical vision of how capital can benefit all when used wisely and appropriately, that is, the realization that there are stakeholders in capital decisions and that their welfare counts. The ability of stakeholders to exit illegitimate enterprises is a fundamental disciplining force in social and economic systems, shaping economic and capital redirection over time (Hirschman 1970; Freeman 2010; Edmans 2011).

Ethical capital is the accumulated institutional capacity to exercise power in ways regarded as legitimate, trustworthy, and oriented toward long-term human flourishing. Capital has a behavioral component, as stakeholders who provide, sustain, and legitimize it exhibit certain behavioral characteristics. They believe in society, organizations, and institutions, and support growth by sustaining and expanding capital. Alternatively, they lose faith and withdraw their support for capital, and society fragments and organizations decay. The elixir of faith in and support for capital growth is grounded in the ethical foundations of society and organizations.

Ethical capital draws on long-standing institutional traditions that govern authority and coordinate collective action, traditions in which dignity functions as a constraint on power rather than a sentiment. Dickens highlighted these traditions and dignities in his imaginative approach to the proper use of capital. These traditions are the enduring sources of ethics that enable institutions to adapt to technological change without forfeiting legitimacy. The arc that spans moral institutional development to the architecture of capital reveals a path to AI governance and use that overcomes Malthusian blind spots. The sections that follow trace the institutional sources of ethical standards and show how ethical capital functions as a governing constraint on AI-enabled systems.

SOURCE OF ETHICAL STANDARDS

Long before modern organizations or advanced technologies, communities faced recurring problems of authority, scale, and unequal influence. Ethical norms developed as practical responses to these conditions, providing shared judgments about restraint, responsibility, and acceptable conduct when formal rules proved incomplete or enforcement imperfect.

Over time, these standards stabilized judgment under uncertainty. Concepts such as virtue, stewardship, and accountability constrain the misuse of power and shape expectations of leadership and fairness. As these norms were reinforced through custom, reputation, and shared practice, they became embedded in professional roles, civic life, and governance structures. Ethics gained traction not by remaining personal or aspirational, but by becoming institutional. In this way, ethical standards reduced uncertainty, enabled delegation, and sustained cooperation even when explicit regulation lagged practice.

In institutional contexts, ethical standards function as capital. They accumulate through consistent conduct, credible leadership, and reinforced norms, shaping how authority is interpreted and whether it is accepted as legitimate. When ethical standards are coherent and widely shared, institutions adapt to change without forfeiting trust. When they fragment or weaken, technical competence and efficiency may persist temporarily while legitimacy erodes. Ethical capacity originates in human capital, formed by experience and responsibility, and is later stabilized through governance and professional norms. As intellectual and structural capital expand through AI-enabled systems, the strength of these ethical foundations becomes increasingly decisive.

Across civilizations, ethical systems emerged not as abstract moral theories but as institutional responses to concentrated power, social vulnerability, and moral risk. These traditions constitute the inherited moral architecture through which societies continue to interpret legitimacy, responsibility, and the rightful exercise of authority.

ETHICAL TRADITIONS AND INSTITUTIONAL ORDER

Classical ethical traditions emerged as institutional responses to enduring problems of authority, legitimacy, and power. Greek philosophy situated ethics in virtue and character rather than in rule compliance alone. Aristotle described ethical behavior as habituated excellence, formed through practice and guided by practical wisdom. Legitimate leadership required deliberation oriented toward the good and action shaped by justice, courage, temperance, and prudence. Ethics functioned as a lived discipline that ordered civic life toward human flourishing rather than as abstract moral instruction (Aristotle 1999).

An AI leadership corollary to Aristotle's notions is essential; it is incongruent for an organization or society to be led by people with underdeveloped ethical capacity while maintaining strong ethical capital. Ethical people shape ethical societies and organizations, which, in turn, create the climate for ethical AI development and use.

Roman thought extended this framework by integrating ethics with law, duty, and institutional stability. Cicero argued that justice and natural law sustained political order and public trust. Law operated not only as coercion but as moral formation, shaping desire and restraining the abuse of power. Virtue remained indispensable, as law detached from moral formation was regarded as ineffective and unstable (Cicero 1999).

This institutional turn toward stability directly applies to modern capital architecture and AI governance. Ethical capital operates through law, duty, and institutional design, shaping how AI is deployed and constraining its use where power would otherwise outrun responsibility.

Christian theology further institutionalized ethics through concepts of moral responsibility, dignity, and stewardship. Augustine and Aquinas framed ethical life as participation in an ordered moral reality that transcended individual preference and political expediency. Authority was entrusted rather than owned, and leadership was accountable to a higher moral order that constrained arbitrary power across generations (Augustine 2003; Aquinas 1947). In the modern period, Pope Leo XIII translated these commitments into social and economic reflection, emphasizing the dignity of labor, the obligations of employers, and the responsibilities of capital as correctives to purely efficiency-driven systems (Leo XIII 1891).

Islamic ethical traditions offer an integrated model of ethics, law, and governance grounded in justice, accountability, and stewardship. Concepts such as justice, trust, and consultation define authority as a moral trust exercised on behalf of the community. Leadership legitimacy depends on fairness, transparency, and protection of the vulnerable, with ethical intent guiding judgment beyond formal compliance (Al-Ghazali 2016; Kamali 2002). Hindu ethical thought offers a complementary framework centered on dharma as moral order and role-based responsibility. Dharma emphasizes discernment, self-restraint, and alignment of action with moral purpose. Leadership is evaluated by the integrity of intention and disciplined action under uncertainty, reflecting the understanding that power exercised without inner restraint destabilizes institutions (Radhakrishnan 1998).

Modern organizational ethics builds on these traditions by treating ethical standards as productive constraints rather than obstacles to performance. Stakeholder theory frames leadership as a responsibility to multiple constituencies whose trust sustains long-term value creation (Freeman 2010). Empirical research on Environmental, Social, and Governance (ESG) and Corporate Social Responsibility (CSR) practices shows that consistent ethical commitments are associated with stronger performance, lower volatility, and greater institutional resilience over time (Berns et al. 2009; Eccles, Ioannou, and Serafeim 2014; Edmans 2011). Across traditions and modern practice, ethical standards serve as social compacts that stabilize judgment, preserve legitimacy, and sustain cooperation when formal rules are incomplete and technical capabilities advance faster than moral clarity.

These traditions explain why ethical standards persist as institutional necessities rather than optional ideals. As moral expectations become embedded in professional norms, governance practices, and reputational consequences, they accumulate and function as capital. Ethical capital captures this accumulated capacity to guide judgment, sustain trust, and legitimate authority when formal rules and technical systems are insufficient. Practices commonly labeled ESG and CSR are best understood as expressions of ethical capital rather than substitutes for it. Framed this way, ethical capital explains how institutions absorb innovation, including AI, without surrendering responsibility or eroding legitimacy.

These ethical traditions establish a consistent pattern. Ethics functions not as an aspiration but as a framework for governance, not as sentiment but as a constraint. Across cultures and institutions, ethical standards emerged to limit how power may be exercised, how capital may be accumulated, and how authority may be delegated. In contemporary organizations, these constraints must operate across daily decisions, institutional design, and the use of AI-enabled systems. Ethics becomes operational when it orders capital in practice rather than in principle, shaping how dignity, responsibility, and judgment are preserved as technology scales.

ETHICS: DIGNITY AS THE ORDERING PRINCIPLE

Ethical traditions exist not to ornament moral theory but to govern power. As organizations adopt AI to manage complexity, speed, and competitive advantage, operational gains can push ethical considerations into the background. Under these conditions, dignity functions not as an abstract ideal but as a practical test of organizational integrity.

Dignity, as embodied in ethical capital, cannot be treated as a mere viewpoint without undermining organizational purpose and social cohesion. When dignity is honored in market and mission-driven choices, and when strong structural capital is guided by ethical capital, ethical societies and organizations become magnets for investment, participation, and long-term commitment (De Soto 2003). Attraction does not require or anticipate perfect societies and organizations, but rather those that strive and demonstrate a concerted commitment to sustainability and stakeholders, and that foster ethical institutions.

A dignity-based focus shapes daily decisions, constrains authority, and determines whether capital formation serves human flourishing or quietly consumes it (Mackey and Sisodia 2014). The framework through which dignity informs capital structure and AI use draws on ethical traditions and is embodied in constitutional and institutional documents that collectively guide how societies and organizations deploy capital.

Dignity is revealed in social documents such as the Magna Carta (1215), which constrained sovereign authority and protected due process; the United States Constitution and Bill of Rights, which safeguard conscience, speech, personhood, and due process; the Universal Declaration of Human Rights, which grounds rights in inherent human dignity; the International Covenant on Civil and Political Rights, which operationalizes those protections; and the Charter of Fundamental Rights of the European Union, whose first article affirms the inviolability of human dignity (Howard 1965; UK Parliament Bill of Rights 1689; United States Congress Bill of Rights 1791; United Nations, Universal Declaration of Human Rights 1948; United Nations, International Covenant on Civil and Political Rights 1966; European Parliament 2000).

The Four Dignities as a Unified Ethical Framework Under AI

From these traditions and documents emerge four distinct yet interrelated dignities that operate together as restraints on power, constructs of social and organizational capital, and guides for AI design and use. Human dignity affirms that persons are not tools, data points, or optimization targets. The dignity of the natural world affirms that creation is a trust across generations rather than an externality of growth. The dignity of space and environment affirms that human flourishing requires humane physical and social conditions. The dignity of free will and conscience affirms that human agency remains personal and cannot be delegated to systems, metrics, or automated processes.

AI use places stress on all four dignities simultaneously. Systems optimized without moral judgment tend to instrumentalize people: data-driven extraction and physical infrastructure strain human and ecological limits. Automated governance reshapes environments at scale. Complex systems that obscure transparency can tempt organizations to shift responsibility from persons to processes. When the four dignities are embedded as constraints within ethical capital structures, they provide a shared ethical vocabulary that enables AI to extend human capability without eroding moral agency. Leaders and stakeholders can envision and test the four dignities.

Each dignity shapes the six forms of capital in distinct ways across families, organizations, communities, and societies. Across legal, philosophical, and theological traditions, dignity emerged as a response to concentrated power. AI represents a new concentration of power, not because it thinks, but because it scales decisions beyond direct human encounter.

ETHICS: A PRODUCTIVE CAPITAL

Ethical capital shapes which actions are deemed legitimate, which behaviors are trusted, and which uses of authority are accepted or resisted. Unlike formal regulation or compliance systems, ethical capital operates where rules are incomplete, enforcement is imperfect, and judgment cannot be avoided.

Ethical capital functions as capital because it produces measurable institutional benefits. Trust lowers transaction costs. Legitimacy enables delegation and coordination. Credibility stabilizes authority during periods of change. Organizations with substantial ethical capital can absorb innovation, withstand errors, and learn from failures without an immediate loss of confidence. Organizations with weak ethical capital may achieve short-term efficiency but incur long-term governance risks and immediate reputational risks.

Structural capital and ethical capital are closely related but distinct. Structural capital governs through laws, policies, procedures, routines, and enforcement mechanisms that formalize authority and allocate decision rights. Ethical capital complements governance by providing direction, meaning, and legitimacy to these structures. Structural capital can compel compliance. Ethical capital attracts participation, sustains consent, and anchors governance in a shared moral purpose.

Ethical capital guides structural capital toward sustainability rather than control alone. It signals which objectives are worthy of pursuit, which trade-offs are acceptable, and which outcomes undermine organizational purpose, even when technically permissible. Without ethical capital, governance structures become vulnerable to extraction, rigidity, or performative compliance. With it, governance gains coherence, adaptability, and stakeholder confidence across changing conditions.

Ethical capital remains distinct from practices commonly associated with ESG standards and CSR. These practices express ethical commitments but do not generate them. Without underlying ethical capital, such initiatives risk fragmentation or instrumental use. Ethical capital provides the normative coherence that enables these practices to function credibly and durably.

The accumulation of ethical capital depends on consistent human behavior and institutional alignment. Credible leadership, shared expectations, and congruence between stated values and observed conduct reinforce it. In environments shaped by AI-enabled systems, ethical capital becomes increasingly decisive.

ETHICAL CAPACITY IS HUMAN CAPITAL

Ethical capital depends on ethical capacity, and ethical capacity resides first within human capital. Organizations do not reason, discern, or exercise conscience independently of the people who design, govern, and operate them. Ethical standards gain force and are sustained only when individuals possess the judgment, responsibility, and moral discipline required to apply them under pressure, ambiguity, and competing incentives.

Ethical capacity is the cultivated ability of individuals to recognize moral stakes, evaluate trade-offs, and act responsibly when rules, metrics, or technical systems provide incomplete guidance or fail to provide ethical clarity. This capacity develops through formation, experience, accountability, and participation in organizational life. It cannot be automated, delegated to systems, or replaced by compliance mechanisms. Ethical capacity is a form of human capital because it is uniquely human, acquired over time, unevenly distributed, and decisive for institutional performance.

The relationship between ethical capacity and ethical capital is reciprocal and reinforcing. Ethical capacity provides the human judgment that ethical capital institutionalizes. Ethical capital, in turn, creates the environment in which ethical capacity is rewarded, modeled, and sustained. Where ethical capacity is weak, ethical capital becomes symbolic or procedural. Where ethical capital is weak, ethical capacity is often discouraged, penalized, or overridden by narrow performance incentives.

When governing leaders establish incentives that encourage short-term gains and foster extractive behaviors, they undermine ethical capital and strain individual ethical capability. The tone at the top undermines sustainable behavior. The organization, society, governing bodies, and stakeholders must be aligned in a mutually reinforcing ethical relationship.

Structural capital interacts with ethical capacity differently. Governance systems allocate authority, specify procedures, and enforce compliance. Ethical capacity shapes how those structures are interpreted and applied in practice. Individuals with strong ethical capacity recognize when rules require discretion, when compliance undermines purpose, and when restraint is necessary despite technical permission. Without ethical capacity, governance becomes rigid, risk-averse, or extractive. With ethical capacity, governance remains adaptive, legitimate, and aligned with institutional purpose.

As AI systems expand, individuals are increasingly asked to rely on outputs that appear objective, efficient, and neutral. Ethical capacity determines whether such outputs are treated as decision support or as substitutes for judgment. When ethical capacity is underdeveloped, responsibility shifts quietly from individuals to systems. When ethical capacity is strong, AI remains embedded within human accountability rather than displacing it.

Organizations that invest in ethical capacity strengthen ethical capital over time. They create conditions in which moral judgment is exercised openly, dissent is permitted, and responsibility remains traceable. These conditions attract stakeholders, sustain trust, and support long-term value creation. Together, ethical capacity and ethical capital form the human and institutional foundations that enable intellectual and structural capital, including AI-enabled systems, to serve a purpose rather than merely optimize performance.

CONTEMPORARY AI ETHICS RESEARCH

Contemporary AI ethics research consistently returns to a common finding. The most persistent risks of AI deployment are not limited to technical performance. They arise from the interaction between AI systems and human judgment within organizations. Ethical capacity, as a form of human capital, determines whether AI functions as decision support and structured automation within accountable governance or becomes a substitute for discernment, weakening responsibility (Floridi et al. 2018; Mittelstadt et al. 2016).

One core area of research concerns bias and disparate impact. Models trained on historical records often reproduce patterns of exclusion embedded in labor markets, lending, policing, healthcare, and education. Social bias arises from historical and ideological data sources, and filtering large datasets is challenging at best. Well-formed and diverse ethical capacity is required to recognize when assumed neutrality produces substantive bias, resulting in a lack of fairness. People must be capable and motivated to uncover AI bias to protect vulnerable groups (Benjamin 2019; Barocas and Selbst 2016).

A second area of concern is a lack of transparency and explainability in AI processes, sources, and outcomes. Many AI systems operate as complex statistical models that are difficult for people to understand or challenge. A system may be difficult to interpret because its internal logic is complex. It may be opaque because vendors limit access to its workings, or it may be opaque because organizations treat AI outputs as final answers without asking for reasons. Ethical capital and capacity are essential to preserve accountability in these situations. Responsible organizations ensure that decision authority is clearly assigned, explanations can be reviewed, and decision thresholds are documented. They also maintain audit trails so that people can override AI systems when necessary, especially in high-stake decisions (Burrell 2016).

A third concern is automation bias and overreliance. Research shows that people often defer to AI recommendations, especially when under time pressure, facing uncertainty, or believing the system has greater expertise. This tendency can reduce questioning and weaken professional judgment. Seasoned human capital with well-honed ethical capacity, supported by ethical capital at the organizational level, counters this risk. It requires human review of important decisions and makes clear that responsibility remains with people, even when AI outputs seem confident or convincing (Parasuraman and Riley 1997; Skitka, Mosier, and Burdick 1999). Users should also have the right to challenge and appeal decisions they believe are wrong.

A fourth concern is value misalignment and distorted goals. AI systems are designed to optimize specific objectives encoded in their training data, feedback loops, and performance metrics. These systems often reward what can be measured, even when those measures conflict with the organization's deeper purpose. This risk is most significant in areas where dignity, meaning, and legitimacy cannot be fully captured by numbers alone. Ethical capacity is needed to check AI outputs through qualitative judgment and human evaluation, not just metrics (Goodhart 1975; Campbell 2011; Mittelstadt 2019).

A fifth concern centers on surveillance, privacy, and power. AI enables large-scale monitoring, prediction, and categorization of people. In workplaces, schools, and public systems, these tools can improve safety and reduce fraud. At the same time, they can normalize control, discourage dissent, and reduce people to data points. Dignity standards and informed ethical capacity are required to judge whether surveillance is proportionate, consensual, and aligned with its stated purpose. Without this capacity, surveillance becomes routine, and trust and legitimacy decline even when systems appear operationally effective (Zuboff 2019; Lyon 2018; Floridi 2019).

Well-developed capital architecture weaves human capital and ethical capacity into a purposeful fabric, supported by a structural, ethical, and intellectual framework that aligns with intent, purposeful incentives, and consistent reinforcement.

INSTITUTIONAL FOUNDATIONS OF AI ETHICS

The ethical governance of AI does not arise from individual organizations acting in isolation. It is shaped by a broader AI environment comprising developers, researchers, consultants, and users that fosters shared concepts, research agendas, standards, and governance frameworks. These institutions do not directly determine ethical outcomes, but they influence how AI systems are designed, evaluated, and integrated into knowledge-based work across sectors (Floridi et al. 2018).

Several research and standards organizations play a central role in this process. The MIT Center for Collective Intelligence examines how humans and machines collaborate in decision-making and problem-solving, emphasizing complementary strengths rather than substitution (Malone 2018). The Stanford Institute for Human-Centered Artificial Intelligence (HAI) (2024) focuses on aligning AI development with human values, social systems, and democratic norms, explicitly framing AI as a sociotechnical system rather than a purely technical artifact (Stanford HAI 2024). The Alan Turing Institute advances research at the intersection of data science, machine learning, and public policy, with particular attention to public-interest and governance applications (Leslie 2019).

International standards bodies also shape the ethical landscape. ISO/IEC JTC 1/SC 42 develops global standards for AI terminology, governance, risk management, and system design, providing shared reference points for organizations operating across jurisdictions (ISO/IEC 2017).

The Organisation for Economic Co-operation and Development (OECD) AI Observatory provides comparative data, policy analysis, and guidance on AI adoption, helping governments and organizations understand how AI affects labor markets, data ecosystems, and institutional capacity (OECD 2024, 2025).

Together, these organizations contribute to the formation of intellectual, ethical, and structural capital in the AI age. They establish standard vocabularies, clarify risk and responsibility categories, and provide frameworks that support coordination across firms, governments, and civil society. Their work reduces fragmentation and promotes organizational learning, especially where formal regulation lags technological change (Floridi 2014).

At the same time, these institutions do not replace ethical judgment. They provide knowledge, standards, and governance tools, but they do not determine how those tools are used in specific contexts. Ethical responsibility remains with human decision-makers and organizational cultures. Frameworks can guide practice, but they cannot replace ethical capacity or ethical capital within an organization (Mittelstadt et al. 2016).

These distinctions lay the groundwork for the triadic framework that follows. Responsible AI use depends not only on technical capability but also on how human and intellectual capital are structured and guided by ethical capital. Without this alignment, effective knowledge use and accountability in society and organizations weaken. With it, AI can be focused on long-term value creation.

THE TRIADIC FRAMEWORK: INTELLECTUAL, STRUCTURAL, AND ETHICAL CAPITAL

At this stage of capital building, it is essential to pause and reflect on the key forms of capital introduced throughout the discussion and consider how they work together to create sustainable value. The framework presented here views AI deployment for human flourishing as governed by three interrelated forms of capital: intellectual, structural, and ethical.

Together, these forms of capital determine whether human capital becomes an effective and responsible agent in organizational value creation, whether stakeholders trust and are willing to engage with an organization's AI systems, and, ultimately, the organization's economic future. This triadic principle also applies to creative and personal human actions. Human actions within an ethical triadic framework enable properly structured incentives to work and foster value creation.

These forms of capital are interdependent. Intellectual capital without an ethical framework risks optimization without purpose. Structural capital without ethical capital encourages compliance without responsibility. Ethical capital without intellectual or structural support articulates values without operational force. Together, the triad ensures coherence and enables careful engagement with the overlapping ethical, educational, and organizational challenges posed by AI.

Intellectual capital encompasses far more than the assets embedded in AI systems. Long before AI, organizations accumulated intellectual capital through the lived experience and judgment of stakeholders, the practical knowledge of supply-chain partners, professional standards and associations, libraries and research institutions, educational institutions, and the collective memory and traditions that shape organizational identity and practice. This human-sourced intellectual capital reflects accumulated insight, error correction, contextual understanding, and moral learning developed over time. In fact, these sources of data and recorded human performance are what AI is trained on.

AI extends existing intellectual capital by adding scale, speed, pattern detection, prediction, and analytical reach. It does not replace or supersede other sources of intellectual capital. AI's value depends on how well it is integrated with, validated against, and disciplined by human knowledge, institutional memory, professional wisdom, and tradition.

By design, intellectual capital is indifferent to purpose, whether drawn from human experience, institutional tradition, or AI-generated analysis. Without ethical direction, human intent, and structural governance, the use of intellectual capital does not necessarily align with the goals of human dignity, fairness, or long-term value. The blending, validation, and orchestration of intellectual capital sources remain irreducibly human responsibilities.

Structural capital provides governance. It defines what may or may not be done and assigns accountability when systems fail. It translates social and organizational expectations into enforceable rules, yet it is necessarily incomplete and often reactive. Formal structures lag technological change and cannot anticipate every ethical dilemma introduced by AI operating at scale.

Ethical capital provides moral purpose and direction aligned with market or mission activities. It guides decision-making and incentives to determine the right course of action. In doing so, ethical capital preserves moral agency, ensuring that dignity is maintained in framing decisions, choices, and incentives.

Within the triadic framework, distinguishing among intellectual, structural, and ethical capital is critical. Each serves a distinct function, and none can substitute for the others without distorting responsibility. Structural capital can enforce compliance without cultivating context, wisdom, or moral obligation. Ethical capital can articulate values without operational force. Intellectual capital can deliver extraordinary capability regardless of purpose.

Responsible AI use reflects triadic alignment. Intellectual capital provides capability. Structural capital imposes constraints. Ethical capital provides direction. Human agency sits at the center of this relationship, interpreting, applying, and, when necessary, restraining both systems and rules. When the triad is aligned, AI amplifies human judgment, sustains institutional trust, and strengthens long-term value creation. When it is misaligned, AI accelerates optimization, while responsibility dissipates into systems, metrics, and procedures.

Triadic Alignment in Practice

Figure 4.1 summarizes the central argument for responsible and effective AI use by illustrating how intellectual, structural, and ethical capital jointly govern it. Each form of capital plays a distinct role, yet none is

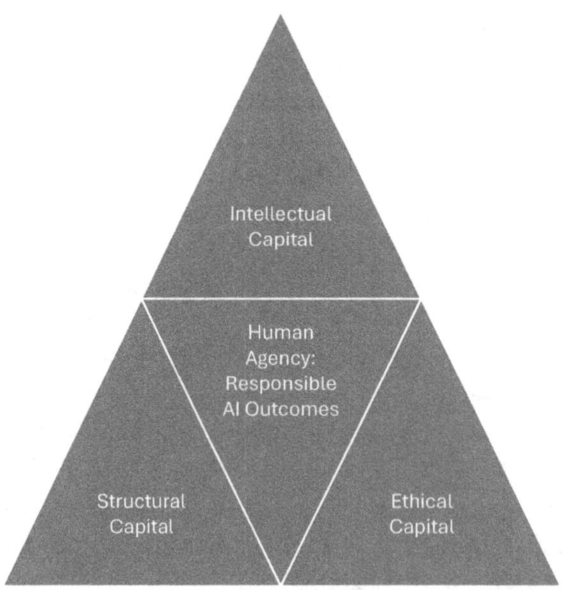

FIGURE 4.1   The triadic capital framework for responsible AI.

sufficient on its own. The relationships depicted in Figure 4.1 emphasize interdependence rather than hierarchy, showing how each form of capital conditions the effectiveness of the others.

Research across disciplines consistently confirms that AI systems must be evaluated by their effects on human agency, dignity, and institutional trust, not solely by technical performance. This growing body of work aligns with the core tenets of the triadic capital framework.

AI Now Institute research shows that, when deployed without adequate ethical and governance constraints, AI systems can amplify existing power imbalances, reshape labor relations, and expand surveillance practices embedded within institutional structures. AI Now's work does not treat these outcomes as isolated technical failures but as consequences of broader governance choices that prioritize scale, speed, or market dominance over accountability and public legitimacy (Zuboff 2019). Across research institutions, standards bodies, and policy frameworks, responsible AI adoption increasingly appears not as a purely technical challenge but as a triadic challenge.

SIDEBAR 4.1   TRIADIC CAPITAL FRAMEWORK AND INSTITUTIONAL PERSPECTIVES ON RESPONSIBLE AI

AI Now Institute

- AI-related risks are often institutional rather than purely technical, stemming from power concentration, governance gaps, and embedded social asymmetries.
- Ethics operates as a form of restraint through accountability, auditability, and the capacity to question, limit, or refuse AI deployments.
- Public legitimacy and democratic oversight are central concerns when AI systems scale authority across social and economic domains.

HAI

- AI should be understood as a socio-technical system embedded within human values, institutions, and social contexts.
- Intellectual capital in the form of models and data requires ethical guidance and human oversight to ensure fairness, trustworthiness, and responsible use.

- Governance, organizational design, and human oversight are critical to shaping ethical outcomes and technical system performance.

OECD AI Observatory and OECD AI Principles (OECD 2024)

- Trustworthy AI is grounded in transparency, accountability, robustness, respect for human rights, and inclusive growth.
- Governance frameworks are necessary to support responsible AI adoption, but they are insufficient without shared ethical norms across jurisdictions.
- Coordination among governments, markets, and civil society depends on ethical capital that builds trust and legitimacy at scale.

ISO/IEC JTC 1/SC 42

- International AI standards formalize terminology, risk-management practices, and governance processes to promote consistency and interoperability.
- Structural capital in the form of standards supports technical alignment but cannot resolve moral judgment or contextual ethical decisions.
- Ethics shapes how standards are interpreted, implemented, and trusted in practice.

MIT Center for Collective Intelligence

- Research examines how humans and AI can collaborate and under what conditions collective intelligence emerges.
- Intellectual capital is most effective when AI augments human judgment and group decision-making rather than replacing them.
- Ethics determines whether human–AI collaboration enhances collective insight or accelerates errors and overconfidence.

Synthesis. Across institutions, perspectives converge on a shared conclusion: responsible AI outcomes emerge when intellectual capital (capability) is governed by structural capital (rules, standards, and accountability mechanisms) and directed by ethical capital (judgment, legitimacy, and restraint). Without this triadic alignment, AI may increase efficiency and scale while eroding trust, accountability, and human agency.

Embedding ethical constraints in AI systems does not eliminate human responsibility; it intensifies the need for moral clarity among system designers, organizational architects, leaders, and decision-makers (Wallach and Allen 2010). A brief review of ethical practices in action shows that organizations are actively experimenting with and revising their AI architectures to meet this responsibility. Taken together, these efforts reveal a discernible movement toward triadic alignment, as organizations seek to coordinate intellectual capability, structural governance, and ethical judgment in practice.

ETHICAL CAPITAL IN PRACTICE

Microsoft and Responsible AI Governance as Ethical Capital in Action

Microsoft illustrates how ethical capital can be deliberately designed into AI governance rather than retrofitted after deployment. Rather than treating ethics as a downstream compliance function or a public relations exercise, Microsoft articulates guiding principles and embeds them directly into organizational governance, technical practice, and accountability structures. In doing so, Microsoft demonstrates that ethical capital operates as a productive form of capital, shaping behavior, preserving trust, and supporting long-term value creation (Microsoft n.d.-b).

Microsoft's Responsible AI framework is organized around six core principles that guide both development and use: fairness, reliability and safety, privacy and security, inclusiveness, transparency, and accountability. Each principle addresses a distinct moral risk associated with AI while reinforcing human responsibility rather than displacing it.

Fairness concerns whether AI systems equitably allocate opportunities, resources, and information across individuals and groups. Rather than assuming AI neutrality, Microsoft requires teams to assess how systems may advantage or disadvantage users along demographic and contextual dimensions. Fairness serves as an ethical norm that shapes design decisions even when legal standards remain ambiguous.

Reliability and safety address the obligation for AI systems to perform consistently across conditions, including contexts beyond those originally anticipated. This principle recognizes that technical accuracy under ideal conditions is insufficient. Ethical and structural capital require resilience, robustness, and foresight, especially when system failures may cause harm. By emphasizing performance across diverse and evolving environments, Microsoft reinforces responsibility for real-world consequences rather than narrow benchmark optimization.

Privacy and security acknowledge that AI systems operate on sensitive data. Microsoft frames privacy not merely as a regulatory requirement but as a moral obligation grounded in respect for human dignity and autonomy. Security safeguards are treated as ethical responsibilities, recognizing that breaches and misuse erode not only user trust but also social trust.

Inclusiveness extends ethical capital beyond risk mitigation to empowerment. Microsoft emphasizes designing systems that are accessible to people with diverse abilities, backgrounds, and circumstances. This approach aligns with stakeholder theory by recognizing that real value creation depends on participation and legitimacy across diverse communities rather than on narrow user segments (Freeman 2010).

Transparency addresses the intelligibility and appropriate use of AI systems. Microsoft emphasizes that users must understand a system's capabilities, limitations, and use context. Transparency is not limited to technical explainability but also includes communication, documentation, and expectation setting. Ethical, structural, and intellectual capital are reflected in a willingness to clarify uncertainty rather than obscure it.

Accountability serves as the keystone principle. Microsoft explicitly affirms that people, not systems, remain responsible for AI outcomes. Oversight mechanisms, escalation pathways, and clearly defined roles ensure that human judgment governs deployment and use. This directly supports the argument that ethical capital preserves moral agency and prevents responsibility from diffusing into infrastructure.

Microsoft operationalizes these principles through an integrated governance model spanning policy, research, and engineering. At the policy level, the company establishes clear rules, standards, and role definitions for responsible AI across business units. At the research level, interdisciplinary teams examine ethical risks, societal impacts, and governance challenges associated with emerging AI capabilities. At the engineering level, responsibility is embedded in design workflows, tooling, and review processes. Employees are expected to act as stewards of responsible AI rather than as passive implementers.

This multilayered approach illustrates how ethical capital differs from and shapes both structural and intellectual capital. Microsoft's framework shows that ethical capital can be intentionally cultivated and scaled without paralyzing innovation. By clarifying responsibility and reinforcing trust, ethical capital reduces long-term risk and strengthens institutional legitimacy.

From a value-creation perspective, Microsoft's Responsible AI governance supports customers by increasing reliability and trust, supports employees by clarifying expectations and accountability, and supports shareholders by reducing exposure to reputational and regulatory shocks. Microsoft's AI approach demonstrates that ethical capital is not an abstract ideal but a strategic asset that shapes how AI-generated value is sustained over time (Microsoft n.d.-b). Microsoft also provides practical implementation resources through its *Embrace Responsible AI Principles and Practices* materials, including learning modules, design guidance, policies, processes, safeguards, and ethical adoption practices (Microsoft n.d.-a).

Unilever and AI Transparency in Human Resources

Unilever's use of AI in recruitment and human resource (HR) management illustrates how ethical capital can be operationalized through transparency, bias mitigation, and sustained human oversight. Unilever publicly discloses how AI is used, retains human decision authority for consequential employment decisions, and audits outcomes for fairness. This approach demonstrates how ethical capital protects organizational legitimacy while preserving operational effectiveness (Eccles et al. 2014; Edmans 2011).

Unilever's stated policy is explicit: "Any decision that has a significant life impact on an individual should not be fully automated" (Davenport and Bean 2023). This principle anchors AI use within human responsibility rather than technical substitution. It reflects ethical capacity and capital as constraints on automation when dignity and long-term human development are at stake.

Thomas Davenport and Randy Bean (2023) describe Unilever's AI ethics approach as a five-stage process that translates ethical intent into organizational practice. Leadership sets the tone and scope through clear ethical commitments. Policies operationalize those commitments across functions. AI use is documented through mechanisms such as model cards. Structured review processes assess adherence to policy and ethical standards. Finally, action determines whether AI systems should be continued, revised, or withdrawn. The critical work occurs in the review and action stages, where organizations decide whether AI applications meet transparency, bias, and fairness standards in practice rather than in principle.

Unilever implements all five stages as part of an integrated ethics system that encompasses tools, services, and HR. Ethical review processes assess not only compliance but also whether AI systems perform as intended and whether they generate unintended effects, including impacts on human capital and internal mobility (Unilever Corporation n.d.). Ethical capital is demonstrated through ongoing evaluation and correction rather than one-time approval.

Through its AI-enabled HR practices, Unilever reached several conclusions that further illuminate the relationship between ethical capital and human capital. Skills development emerged as a strategic priority, with reskilling existing employees often proving more effective and less costly than external hiring. AI-supported talent mobility was recognized as a way to empower individuals to shape their careers rather than as a tool for rigid classification.

Bias mitigation was treated as an ethical objective requiring continuous oversight rather than as a purely technical fix. Cultural change was identified as necessary, and upskilling was framed as a competitive and institutional imperative. Finally, cross-industry collaboration was recognized as essential, reflecting the view that workforce transitions cannot be addressed by individual firms acting alone (Unilever Corporation n.d.). Unilever's experience highlights that ethical capital supports transparency, preserves legitimacy, and strengthens human capital when AI is integrated into core organizational functions.

IBM, Amazon, and the Limits of Explainability: Ethical Capital as Restraint

IBM offers a clear example of ethical capital expressed through restraint rather than technological expansion. In June 2020, the company announced that it would no longer sell, develop, or offer general-purpose facial recognition or analysis software (Peters 2020). The decision was communicated publicly by the CEO Arvind Krishna in a letter to members of the U.S. Congress, which emphasized opposition to uses of the technology for mass surveillance, racial profiling, and other applications inconsistent with principles of trust and transparency. IBM also called for broader public dialogue and regulatory engagement regarding the use of such technologies by law enforcement and public agencies (Reuters Staff 2020).

IBM's decision reflected recognition that technical improvements alone cannot address deeper ethical concerns. They are insufficient when the underlying use raises questions about privacy, civil liberties, racial justice, and institutional legitimacy. Technically sophisticated facial recognition technologies raise social value issues that extend beyond engineering performance and require collective ethical judgment before deployment.

Amazon reached a similar conclusion in 2021, when it extended its moratorium on law enforcement use of facial recognition software amid sustained concern from civil and human rights organizations (Reuters Staff 2021). Like IBM, Amazon acknowledged that the absence of clear governance frameworks and shared societal standards made continued deployment ethically problematic, despite technical capability.

Viewed through the triadic capital framework, these decisions illustrate how ethical capital serves as a governing force when intellectual and structural capital prove insufficient. Intellectual capital enabled the continued research, development, and commercialization of facial recognition technologies. Structural capital, in the absence of comprehensive regulation and ethical considerations, permitted market deployment. Ethical considerations reframed market choices by asking whether specific AI applications should proceed at all, given their implications for dignity, justice, and public trust. In each case, ethical judgment constrained technical possibility and market incentive.

For organizational leaders and policymakers, the IBM and Amazon cases underscore a critical lesson in AI governance. Responsible leadership sometimes requires not scaling or pursuing technologies until adequate oversight, accountability, and shared ethical standards are in place. Ethical capital is expressed not only through proactive design and governance but also through principled refusal and restraint. Such restraint preserves legitimacy, protects institutional trust, and signals that human judgment, rather than technical feasibility alone, governs the boundaries of acceptable AI use.

TRIADIC ALIGNMENT AND INSTITUTIONAL CONSEQUENCES

Ethical issues in AI are most evident when systems focus on narrow metrics at the expense of human goals. In healthcare, systems that maximize reimbursement often enhance billing but do not necessarily improve patient health outcomes (Bradlow, Werner, and Asch 2008). For example, a commonly used population-health algorithm intended to allocate care efficiently has consistently underserved Black patients because it used care costs as an indicator of clinical need (Obermeyer et al. 2019).

In public policy, predictive policing and risk-assessment tools tend to reinforce historical inequities because they focus on biased past patterns instead of current realities or ethical goals (Lum and Isaac 2016). Evidence across different fields shows that prioritizing a specific metric often leads to outcomes that are undesirable and sometimes unfair. Metrics that lack a clear purpose or ethical considerations distort the work they are supposed to inform.

Empirical studies on ESG and CSR confirm this. Companies that incorporate ethical values into their strategy and operations tend to show better financial results, less volatility, and enhanced resilience during challenging times (Clark, Feiner, and Viehs 2015; Friede, Busch, and Bassen 2015). These advantages are especially significant when ethical principles are a fundamental part of value creation rather than mere symbolic gestures.

Organizations that implement AI transparently, honor stakeholder dignity, and invest in responsible practices build trust. This trust leads to customer loyalty, engaged employees, and confident investors (Porter and Kramer 2011; Mayer 2019). Ethical capital is not a cost but a stabilizing element that enhances value creation.

Ethical capital guides AI innovation rather than restricting it. It aligns intellectual and structural resources with goals that uphold human agency, dignity, and trust in institutions. Viewing AI as a form of intellectual capital rooted in intentional structural and ethical principles helps create a clear framework for responsible implementation.

TAKEAWAYS

- AI functions as and expands intellectual capital, extending analytical capability and scale, but remains indifferent to purpose without guidance.

- Structural capital provides governance, rules, and accountability, but cannot anticipate every ethical dilemma or substitute for judgment.

- Ethical capital guides action when compliance is insufficient, preserving human agency and institutional legitimacy.

- Responsible AI outcomes emerge only when intellectual, structural, and ethical capital align.

- Metric optimization without an ethical purpose yields distorted and often unjust outcomes, even when technically effective.

- Ethical capital is not a constraint on innovation but a stabilizing force that supports trust, resilience, and long-term value creation.

- AI magnifies ethical failure and requires ethical standards, making governance choices more consequential, not less.

- The governance of AI is ultimately an institutional and moral challenge, not merely a technical matter.

WORKS CITED

Aquinas, Thomas. 1947. *Summa Theologica*. Translated by Fathers of the English Dominican Province. New York: Benziger Bros.

Aristotle. 1999. *Nicomachean Ethics* (2nd ed.). Translated by Terence Irwin. New York: Hackett Publishing Company, Inc.

Augustine. 2003. *City of God*. Translated by Henry Bettenson. London, UK: Penguin Books.

Barocas, Solon, and Andrew D. Selbst. 2016. "Big Data's Disparate Impact." *California Law Review* 104 (3): 671–732. http://www.jstor.org/stable/24758720

Benjamin, Ruha. 2019. *Race After Technology: Abolitionist Tools for the New Jim Code*. Medford, MA: Polity Press.

Berns, Maurice, Andrew Townend, Zayna Khayat, Balu Balagopal, Martin Reeves, Michael S. Hopkins, and Nina Kruschwitz. 2009. "Sustainability and Competitive Advantage." *MIT Sloan Management Review* 51 (1): 19–26.

Bradlow, Eric T., Rachel M. Werner, and David A. Asch. 2008, April 1. "Hospital Performance Measures and Quality of Care." Vers. Volume 13, Number 5. *Scholarly Commons*. Leonard Davis Institute of Health Issue Brief Economics. Accessed December 26, 2025. https://repository.upenn.edu/entities/publication/4d7c7e33-3ac7-4f8e-9366-b66d19de900f

Burrell, Jenna. 2016. "How the Machine 'Thinks:' Understanding Opacity in Machine Learning Algorithms." *Big Data & Society* 3 (1). Accessed January 5, 2026. https://papers.ssrn.com/sol3/papers.cfm?abstract_id=2660674

Campbell, Donald T. 2011. "Assessing the Impact of Planned Social Change." *Journal of Multidisciplinary Evaluation* 7 (15): 3–43.

Cicero, Marcus Tullius. 1999. *On the Commonwealth and On the Laws*. Cambridge Texts in the History of Political Thought. Translated by James E. G. Zetzel. Cambridge: Cambridge University Press.

Clark, Gordon L., Andreas Feiner, and Michael Viehs. 2015, March 5. "From the Stockholder to the Stakeholder: How Sustainability Can Drive Financial Outperformance." *SSRN*. Accessed December 26, 2025. https://papers.ssrn.com/sol3/papers.cfm?abstract_id=2508281

Davenport, Thomas H., and Randy Bean. 2023, November 15. *MIT Sloan Management Review*. Accessed December 22, 2025. https://sloanreview.mit.edu/article/ai-ethics-at-unilever-from-policy-to-process

De Soto, Hernando. 2003. *The Mystery of Capital: Why Capitalism Triumphs in the West and Fails Everywhere Else*. New York: Basic Books.

Dickens, Charles. 2008. *A Christmas Carol*. London, UK: Puffin Books.

Eccles, Robert G., Ioannis Ioannou, and George Serafeim. 2014. "The Impact of Corporate Sustainability on Organizational Processes and Performance." *Management Science* 60 (11): 2835–2857.

Edmans, Alex. 2011. "Does the Stock Market Fully Value Intangibles? Employee Satisfaction and Equity Prices." *Journal of Financial Economics* 101 (3): 621–640.

European Parliament. 2000, December 18. "Charter of Fundamental Rights of the European Union." *Official Journal of the European Communities*. Accessed January 12, 2026. https://www.europarl.europa.eu/charter/pdf/text_en.pdf

Floridi, Luciano. 2014. *The Fourth Revolution: How the Infosphere Is Reshaping Human Reality* (1st ed.). Oxford: Oxford University Press.

Floridi, Luciano. 2019. "Establishing the Rules for Building Trustworthy AI." *Nature Machine Intelligence* 1: 261–262.

Floridi, Luciano, Josh Cowl, Monica Beltrametti, Raja Chatila, Patrice Chazerand, Virginia Dignum, Christoph Luetge, Robert Madelin, Ugo Pagallo, Francesca Rossi, Burkhard Schafer, Peggy Valcke, and Effy Vayena. 2018. "AI4People – An Ethical Framework for a Good AI Society: Opportunities, Risks, Principles, and Recommendations." *Minds and Machines* 28: 689–707.

Freeman, R. Edward. 2010. *Strategic Management: A Stakeholder Approach*. Cambridge: Cambridge University Press.

Friede, Gunnar, Timo Busch, and Alexander Bassen. 2015. "ESG and Financial Performance: Aggregated Evidence from More than 2000 Empirical Studies." *Journal of Sustainable Finance & Investment* 5 (4): 210–233.

Ghazali, Abu Hamid Al. 2016. *The Book of Knowledge*. Translated by Kenneth Honerkamp. Vol. 1, 40 vols. Louisville, KY: Fons Vitae.

Goodhart, Charles A. E.. 1975. "Problems of Monetary Management: The UK Experience." Papers in *Monetary Economics*. Reserve Bank of Australia: 1–20.

Hirschman, Albert O. 1970. *Exit, Voice, and Loyalty: Responses to Decline in Firms, Organizations, and States*. Cambridge, MA: Harvard University Press.

Howard, A. E. D. 1965. *Magna Carta: Text and Commentary*. Charlottesville, VA: University of Virginia Press.

ISO/IEC JTC 1/SC 42. 2017. "Artificial Intelligence." *ISO*. Accessed January 9, 2026. https://www.iso.org/committee/6794475.html

Kamali, Mohammad Hashim. 2002. *Freedom, Equality and Justice in Islam*. Cambridge, UK: Islamic Texts Society.

Leo XIII. 1891, May 15. *Rerum Novarum*. Vatican City: Libreria Editrice Vaticana.

Leslie, David. 2019. "Understanding Artificial Intelligence Ethics and Safety: A Guide for the Responsible Design and Implementation of AI Systems in the Public Sector." *The Alan Turing Institute*. Accessed January 9, 2026. https://www.turing.ac.uk/sites/default/files/2019-08/understanding_artificial_intelligence_ethics_and_safety.pdf

Lum, Kristian, and William Isaac. 2016, October. "To Predict and Serve?" *Significance* 7: 14–19.

Lyon, David. 2018. *The Culture of Surveillance: Watching as a Way of Life.* Cambridge, UK: Polity Press.

Mackey, John, and Raj Sisodia. 2014. *Conscious Capitalism: Liberating the Heroic Spirit of Business.* Boston, MA: Harvard Business Review Press.

Malone, Thomas W. 2018. *Superminds: The Surprising Power of People and Computers Thinking Together.* New York: Little, Brown Spark.

Malthus, Thomas Robert. 2018. *An Essay on the Principle of Population.* New Haven, CT: Yale University Press.

Mayer, Colin. 2019. *Prosperity: Better Business Makes the Greater Good.* Oxford: Oxford University Press.

Microsoft. n.d.-a *Embrace Responsible AI Principles and Practices.* Accessed December 22, 2025. https://learn.microsoft.com/en-us/training/modules/embrace-responsible-ai-principles-practices

Microsoft. n.d.-b *Microsoft Responsible AI: Tools and Practices.* Accessed December 11, 2025. https://www.microsoft.com/en-us/ai/tools-practices

Mittelstadt, Brent. 2019. "Principles Alone Cannot Guarantee Ethical AI." *Nature Machine Intelligence* 1 (11): 501–507. doi: 10.1038/s42256-019-0114-4

Mittelstadt, Brent Daniel, Patrick Allo, Mariarosaria Taddeo, Sandra Wachter, and Luciano Floridi. 2016. "The Ethics of Algorithms: Mapping the Debate." *Big Data & Society* 3 (2). doi: 10.1177/2053951716679679

Obermeyer, Ziad, Brian Powers, Christine Vogeli, and Sendhil Mullainathan. 2019, October. "Dissecting Racial Bias in an Algorithm Used to Manage the Health of Populations." *Science* 25: 447–453.

OECD. 2024. "AI Principles." *OECD.* Accessed January 10, 2026. https://www.oecd.org/en/topics/sub-issues/ai-principles.html

OECD. 2025, September 18. *Governing with Artificial Intelligence: The State of Play and Way Forward in Core Government Functions.* Accessed January 1, 2026. https://www.oecd.org/en/publications/2025/06/governing-with-artificial-intelligence_398fa287/full-report/ai-in-fighting-corruption-and-promoting-public-integrity_60f5c50a.html

Parasuraman, Raja, and Victor Riley. 1997. "Humans and Automation." *Human Factors* 39 (2): 230–253.

Peters, Jay. 2020, June 8. "IBM Will No Longer Offer, Develop, or Research Facial Recognition Technology." *The Verge.* Accessed December 26, 2025. https://www.theverge.com/2020/6/8/21284683/ibm-no-longer-general-purpose-facial-recognition-analysis-software?utm_source=chatgpt.com

Porter, Michael E., and Mark R. Kramer. 2011. "Creating Shared Value." *Harvard Business Review* 89 (1/2): 62–77.

Radhakrishnan, S. 1998. *Indian Philosophy.* Vol. 2, 2 vols. New York/New Delhi: Oxford University Press.

Reuters Staff. 2020, June 9. "IBM Will No Longer Offer Facial Recognition Technology and Opposes Use for Racial Profiling." *World Economic Forum.* Accessed December 26, 2025. https://www.weforum.org/stories/2020/06/ibm-facial-recognition-george-floyd/?utm_source=chatgpt.com

Reuters Staff. 2021, May 18. "Amazon Extends Moratorium on Police Use of Facial Recognition Software; Rights Groups Call for Permanent Ban." *Business and Human Rights Centre.* Accessed December 26, 2025. https://www.business-humanrights.org/en/latest-news/amazon-extends-moratorium-on-police-use-of-facial-recognition-software-rights-groups-call-for-permanent-ban

Skitka, Linda J., Kathleen L. Mosier, and Mark Burdick. 1999. "Does Automation Bias Decision-Making?" *International Journal of Human-Computer Studies* 51 (5): 991–1006.

Stanford Institute for Human-Centered Artificial Intelligence (HAI). 2024. "Human-Centered AI: Annual Report." *Stanford University.* Accessed January 9, 2026. https://hai.stanford.edu/about/annual-reports

UK Parliament. 1689, December. "Bill of Rights 1689." *UK Parliament.* Accessed January 12, 2026. https://www.parliament.uk/about/living-heritage/evolutionofparliament/parliamentaryauthority/revolution/collections1/collections-glorious-revolution/billofrights

Unilever Corporation. n.d. *The Future of Skills: Using Tech to Put People First.* Accessed December 22, 2025. https://www.unilever.com/news/news-search/2021/the-future-of-skills-using-tech-to-put-people-first

United Nations. 1948, December 10. "Universal Declaration of Human Rights." *United Nations.* Accessed January 12, 2026. Paris: United Nations General Assembly. Adopted December 10, 1948.

United Nations. 1966, December 16. "International Covenant on Civil and Political Rights." *United Nations.* Accessed January 12, 2026. https://www.ohchr.org/en/instruments-mechanisms/instruments/international-covenant-civil-and-political-rights

United States Congress. 1791. "National Archives." *Bill of Rights.* Accessed January 12, 2026. https://www.archives.gov/milestone-documents/bill-of-rights

Wallach, Wendell, and Colin Allen. 2010. *Moral Machines: Teaching Robots Right from Wrong.* Oxford, UK: Oxford University Press.

Zuboff, Shoshana. 2019. *The Age of Surveillance Capitalism: The Fight for a Human Future at the New Frontier of Power.* New York: Public Affairs.

CHAPTER 5

Structures and Boundaries That Promote AI Creativity, Productivity, and Innovation

UNDERSTANDING THE BOUNDARIES OF ARTIFICIAL AND AUTHENTIC WORLDS

Contrary to a popular myth, art, discovery, and creative imagination are not fostered by unstructured processes. Disciplines and structures scaffold all inquiry and enable a flow of productive energy. Creativity, productivity, and innovation are not unleashed by removing boundaries but by aligning structural capital with human judgment and ethical purpose. Every transformative technology extends human possibility by reorganizing the structures through which intention, authority, and responsibility are exercised.

The printing press made knowledge portable by reshaping institutions of learning, authorship, and authority. Electricity extended productive life beyond daylight by restructuring work, time, and urban space. The Internet has collapsed how intellectual assets are accessed, how distance

DOI: 10.1201/9781003744061-5

and geography separate access, and how long it takes to engage with information, knowledge, and data by redesigning communication channels, markets, and social connections. In each case, the enduring effects of the technology depended on how structural capital governed and bounded its creation, use, and implementation, through governing laws, professional norms, organizational roles, accountability mechanisms, and institutional design that translated new capabilities into a new ordering (Winner 1980[1]; Ellul 1964[2]).

When technological capability advances faster than stabilizing structures, the result is structural anarchy, leading to uncertainty about the role of artificial intelligence (AI). Douglass North (1990) argues that institutions exist to reduce uncertainty in human interaction by providing stable constraints that shape incentives and expectations, reducing structural anarchy. When those constraints are absent or underdeveloped, economic and social activity becomes vulnerable to exploitation, advantage-seeking behavior, and the erosion of trust.

Across professional and intellectual disciplines, structural capital is understood as the institutional framework that governs the mobilization, constraints, and coordination of capability at scale. Whether described as the organizational architecture that retains intellectual capital beyond individuals (Roos and Roos 1997), the embedded residue of knowledge in systems and routines (Stewart 1997), the humanly devised constraints that reduce uncertainty and structure social and economic interaction (North 1990), or the cultural norms and shared meanings that condition economic outcomes over time (Throsby 2001), these perspectives converge on a common insight: capability becomes value-producing, productive, and legitimate only when embedded within institutional structures that align authority, responsibility, and purpose.

AI research and contemporary philosophy of information consistently distinguish networked performance from the structured, bounded human capacity to harness understanding, meaning, and alignment to achieve responsible action. These distinctions warn against conflating fluent output with structured human capacity and against confusing probability with purpose or data with insights (Russell and Norvig 2021; Floridi and Chiriatti 2020).

When an AI-enhanced robot with advanced sensors and mechanics makes an error, the blame is placed on its programming, sensor function, or mechanical performance. It is reprogrammed, refitted, and fixed. Its use and limits must always be clearly defined and not confused with human agency. For this reason, the Turing Test no longer provides an adequate benchmark. Technology has advanced to the point that it mimics human performance with a level of sophistication that blurs the distinction between mimicry and sentience.

SIDEBAR 5.1   THE TURING TEST AND THE LIMITS OF IMITATION

- Alan Turing's imitation game, commonly called the Turing Test, was designed to determine whether a machine could produce conversational responses indistinguishable from those of a human. It was not intended to assess understanding, judgment, or moral agency.
- Passing the Turing Test demonstrates behavioral resemblance, not comprehension of meaning, awareness of consequences, or responsibility for outcomes.
- Contemporary AI systems can generate fluent language, images, and decisions that closely resemble human output, often at remarkable speed and scale. These capabilities reflect advances in pattern recognition and statistical prediction, not the presence of intention or understanding.
- Imitation remains categorically distinct from agency. AI systems do not know why an answer matters, cannot evaluate consequences in moral terms, and do not bear responsibility for errors, misuse, or harm.
- Treating imitation as intelligence risks delegating judgment to systems that cannot be held accountable, undermining human authorship, responsibility, and ethical oversight. The Turing Test illustrates how structural anarchy arises when imitation is treated as agency.
- The value of AI lies not in replacing human agency but in supporting it. Recognizing the limits of imitation helps preserve creativity, judgment, and responsibility within organizations, ensuring that decision-making remains grounded in human purpose rather than in automated plausibility.

Disruptive technologies routinely emerge faster than human institutions can absorb them. However, significant disruption is not inevitable. It can be mitigated through intentional education, a coherent organizational vision, and public policy that anticipates technological change rather than responding only after consequences become visible.

AI occupies a distinctive, wedge-shaped space within this disruption ecology. It serves as an instrument of intellectual leverage, enabling smaller groups or individuals to perform tasks once reserved for far larger organizations (Brynjolfsson and McAfee 2016). For better or worse, AI's effects hinge on those who design, deploy, and govern it.

An example helps ground this seeming dichotomy between disruptive and supportive. An advanced-level photographer wants to capture a perfect snapshot of lightning in the mountains, with snow and diffused lighting. The creative and structured imagination knows what image is extraordinary, the photographer's. An AI-enabled sensing and adjusting tool linked to the camera senses and adjusts the camera at speeds and with predesigned parameters that humans cannot match. The shot is architected by the photographer, timed and adjusted by an AI-enabled device, and refined in AI-enabled post-production software that brings the image to near perfection. The right balance of creative boundaries is established through human intuition and experience, and AI gets the camera snap just right. If the photographer desires, this photo can become part of the explicit body of data that AI can reuse, provided the appropriate copyright, disclosure, and fee rules are in place.

Boundaries are not constraints on possibility but frames of envisioned prudence. They ensure that technological power does not outrun judgment. Boundaries protect dignity, clarify intention, and orient systems toward the common good rather than toward extraction or manipulation. Without such limits, creativity collapses into imitation, innovation becomes disruption without direction, and productivity yields speed without meaning (Jonas 1985). Prudence advances development in stages, allowing reflection and accountability to keep pace with capability. These boundaries mark the terrain on which the future of AI will be determined.

BOUNDARIES: MEASURING AND ALIGNING

Every organization holds a portfolio of capital. Some forms are tangible, others relational, and others remain invisible to standard accounting systems. Each form contributes to human accomplishment, organizational value creation, and social well-being. Yet, each form of capital either grows or decays, depending on how it is cultivated, protected, and aligned.

Consider the six forms of capital. Each serves a distinct function, yet none operates in isolation. When leaders prioritize a single form, such as financial returns or technological sophistication, the others often erode quietly. Changes to any one form require intentional design, shared understanding, and careful restructuring to ensure that capability is strengthened rather than diminished. The architecture of capital is an essential human endeavor, and structural capital provides the toolkit to align, incentivize, and orchestrate capital to support creative and productive activities.

AI intensifies these architectural and structural demands. AI introduced without careful harmonization and structuring across the six forms of capital can hollow out the very capacities it is intended to enhance. In this AI-deployed context, boundaries are the decision criteria, governance thresholds, and evaluative processes that determine whether and how new technologies are introduced in ways that strengthen performance and desirable outcomes.

Boundaries are not constraints for their own sake. They encourage leaders to determine whether new technologies deepen service, steward human dignity, and build long-term capability, or merely chase novelty, spin toward the mirage of magical cost reductions, and portray symbolic progress. These short-term impulses often weaken the organizational and social foundations that support the capital pillars that sustain long-term value creation.

Leaders and community members should ask the *why, how, when, and process* questions, and assess changes to capital and mission capabilities with sobriety, clarity, and research before implementation. To move wisely, leaders and affected stakeholders should first understand the capabilities they already possess and how they are structured for proper use. They should measure the strength and trajectory of each capital form, identify where decay is already occurring, and define the desired future state. Only then can technology, including AI, be budgeted, governed, and deployed as a servant rather than a master.

It may seem trite, but effective technology leadership requires the ability to articulate the purpose, use, limits, and outcomes of new technologies before implementation. Articulation should not be a vague notion of the current state of capital, operations, and outcomes, but a clear vision grounded in capacity, need, and use. The distinction between vague dreaming and clear envisioning is critical to the proper architecture of capital and boundary setting. Unstructured aspirations risk structural anarchy, and structured, disciplined envisioning enhances thoughtful structural building.

The goal is not merely to add AI and hope for better outcomes. The goal is to achieve a net increase across all six forms of capital, especially human capital, the source of returns. This requires intentional discipline. Leaders must learn to conduct capital inventories, design multicapital budgets, and align investments with an explicit, envisioned future that prioritizes human flourishing. This is a disciplined, meaning-making, applied, impact-focused, measure-rich, and managed process.

The following checklist provides a practical tool for harmonizing structures, aligning capital, and applying the principles of structured envisioning.

CHECKLIST: HARMONIZING THE SIX CAPITALS BEFORE ADOPTING AI

1. Inventory: Where Are We Now?

Human Capital

- ☐ Have people developed the skills, knowledge, abilities, and behaviors needed to use the current capital stock and implement AI (possess the appropriate stock of human capital)?

- ☐ Are people currently suffering from burnout, turnover, or disengagement, and does adding AI add to that suffering, or does it mitigate the causes (maintenance of human capital)?

- ☐ Are teams and key stakeholders trusted, mentored, valued, and given opportunities to share insights on current and future state capital and AI usage (engaging human capital)?

Intellectual Capital

- ☐ What knowledge, intellectual processes, models, and insights define current societal or organizational work (the value of current intellectual capital)?

- ☐ Is critical expertise concentrated in too few people or systems (underutilization of intellectual capital and overreliance on tacit or system-bound knowledge)?

☐ Does the current intellectual capital system capture, document, and share individual and organizational learning, making know-what, know-how, and know-why explicit (across tacit and explicit knowledge boundaries)?

Structural Capital

☐ Are policies, governance, and accountability clear, compelling, and just (for value creation and sustainability)?

☐ Do decision rights support responsibility and transparency (accountability)?

☐ Are capital and performance governance systems resilient? Can these systems withstand, correct, and realign in response to disruption rather than merely accelerating it (AI pre-implementation priority)?

Physical Capital

☐ Are facilities (including outsourced facilities), tools, and physical infrastructure safe, efficient, and resilient?

☐ Are upgrades pursued for need, not for trend? Do they align with the organization's vision and value-creation strategies?

Financial Capital

☐ Are financial resources stable, ethical, and sustainable? Do they demonstrate knowledge of risk and rewards and communicate value creation effectively?

☐ Are investments aligned with the mission, vision, values, and people?

Ethical Capital

☐ Do decisions embody virtue, trust, and ethical clarity? Do they shape ethical capital that attracts or repels stakeholders?

☐ Are stakeholders treated with dignity? Do the leaders and members of the organization have the appropriate vision of dignity?

☐ Do practices align with stated and revealed values?

2. Budgeting for Capital and AI: Are We Investing Wisely?

Before Funding AI, Leaders Should Ask:

- ☐ Which capital is most vulnerable right now, and why?

- ☐ Does AI risk accelerate decay (e.g., deskilling workers or weakening stakeholder trust)?

- ☐ Is budgeting used to strengthen human, structural, intellectual, and ethical capital alongside technology (Triadic approach)?

- ☐ Do training, governance, and formation plans exist for AI implementation, not just for hardware and software? If there is capital displacement, redundancies, or restructuring, are there plans to support those affected? Do plans reflect organizational or social values, and do they consider employees, families, communities, customers, supply chain partners, and other stakeholders who contribute to value creation (value creation is the result of processes or actions that support sustainable market or mission accomplishment at a defined and recognized level)?

- ☐ Where should investment precede AI, such as in leadership development, culture, or mission clarity?

If AI requires sacrificing formation, relationships, or human capability, it may not yet be the right investment.

3. Alignment with Envisioned Future State

Envisioned Future Questions:

- ☐ What kind of society or organization do we aspire to be?

- ☐ What kind of people do we hope to form?

- ☐ How does technology serve that identity?

- ☐ What do we refuse to lose: dignity, trust, presence, and formation?

- ☐ If AI disappeared tomorrow, would our organization remain strong?

Candid assessment and the actions required to establish boundaries and align require courage. It means choosing investments that deepen vocation, strengthen service, and sustain the six forms of capital, even when faster or more glamorous paths seem available. When boundaries are clear and people are well prepared, AI becomes a partner rather than an imagined quick fix. When the forms of capital are harmonized, innovation matures. When leaders value dignity, the other forms of capital fall into proper order. These considerations reflect aspirations disciplined by wisdom. AI can be a massive multiplier or a disastrous distraction. Thoughtful implementation determines the trajectory. The appropriate governance structure can make the difference between a multiplier and a disaster.

AI: STEWARDSHIP, TRUST, AND GOVERNANCE

In many domains, AI is already doing extraordinary work. Adaptive learning systems personalize education, reducing barriers for students who might otherwise fall behind. Clinicians use AI-assisted diagnostics to interpret scans more accurately and identify diseases earlier. Logistics systems predict demand, reduce waste, and conserve energy. Public administrators apply analytics to streamline services and expose corruption. Properly designed, these tools expand human ingenuity and help build what may be described as ethically aligned structural capital: the proper boundaries animated by accumulated trust, reliability, and civic goodwill that enable organizations and societies to function at their best (Brynjolfsson and McAfee 2016; Topol 2019).

Yet, the same leverage that generates benefits can also accelerate harm. Recent years have seen rapid growth in deepfakes, synthetic identities, sophisticated fraud, and coordinated disinformation. Audio and video can now be fabricated with such realism that citizens increasingly struggle to distinguish genuine from artificially produced content. Criminal networks automate phishing, identity theft, and financial deception. Bad-faith political actors manipulate social divisions through precision-targeted misinformation. Even well-intentioned organizations sometimes deploy automated decision systems that quietly encode bias or reduce people to data categories that lack context and humanity (O'Neil 2016; Europol 2024; Tufekci 2015).

The first commitment is to deploy AI in ways guided by prudence, transparency, fairness, and genuine human benefit. Structures and boundaries are shaped by the question: *Can AI be used effectively to create value, and how should it be structured?* This question prompts ethical alignment: *Should this be done, and who does it ultimately serve?*

The second commitment recognizes that AI can reinforce structural capital. The same sophistication that creates risk can also protect against it. AI now helps identify financial fraud, flag manipulated images and videos, trace coordinated disinformation networks, and detect malicious cyber behavior before it spreads widely (Pilati and Venturini 2025; Heim, Anderljung, and Belfield 2024). Clear boundaries, guided by accountability, law, and transparent oversight, help societies and organizations preserve openness and freedom.

Some societies have also established boundary mechanisms, such as the 2024 European Union's Artificial Intelligence Act (EU AI Act), which regulates and requires good-faith disclosure when end users interact with AI, including chatbots and deepfakes. The EU AI Act website provides historical information and guidance for small- and medium-sized business users to help protect against AI misuse. In the United States, the back-and-forth between first-mover innovation in AI and restrictive use has led to limited government oversight and regulation. This may change as the threat environment evolves. While formal regulation establishes necessary external boundaries, the deeper and more enduring work of boundary setting occurs within organizations and individuals, where intellectual capital is formed, cultivated, and directed toward creative and purposeful activity.

AI: Intellectual Capital Bounded Value Creation

Intellectual capital, properly bounded, enhances creativity in at least four ways.

1. Allowing thinkers to focus on higher-order meaning. Lower-order cognitive tasks are more readily delegated to AI to capture intellectual capital. This plays to human capital strengths by enabling humans to focus on what is uniquely human: creating, innovating, experimenting, judging, and ethical applications.

2. Expands accessible knowledge through broader, deeper scanning and screening of the horizon of what can be explored. This approach leverages AI's strengths in data access, review, and probability-of-match assessment.

3. Supports collaboration by synchronizing expertise across domains, addressing governance needs for structural capital, and optimizing financial and physical capital.

4. Reduces time-on-task requirements and enhances creative and innovative thinking.

When AI contributes well-structured intellectual capital, it can deepen the conditions that make creative flow possible: clarity of goals, immediate feedback, manageable challenge, and alignment of effort with the stated purpose (Csikszentmihalyi 1996). Mihaly Csikszentmihalyi describes flow as the state in which concentration, mastery, and meaning converge, producing deep engagement and creative energy. AI does not generate creativity, but it can remove distractions, assist focus by responding within established boundaries, reduce superficial work, alleviate time pressure, and expand access to foundational knowledge, enabling this flow state to emerge more consistently.

Creativity, however, is more than productivity or novelty. Teresa Amabile (1996) defines creativity as work that is both novel and appropriate, arising from the interaction of expertise, creative-thinking skills, and intrinsic motivation. Keith Sawyer (2012) emphasizes that creativity is often collaborative and iterative, emerging from social contexts rather than from solitary inspiration. Robert Sternberg (1988) emphasizes that creativity requires the courage to challenge convention, the wisdom to evaluate ideas realistically, and the ethical awareness to pursue creativity in the service of the common good. Together, these perspectives reveal creativity as a living process shaped by the structured integration of knowledge, community, conscience, and disciplined effort. Csikszentmihalyi's concept of flow captures the inner experience of this process, in which attention, challenge, mastery, and meaning align within facilitating boundaries.

Used wisely, AI can organize information, provide rapid feedback, and free up human cognitive space for higher-order thinking. In doing so, it enables human capital to operate more effectively and can support creative flow by expanding the range of possibilities available to human agency. The creative act itself, however, remains human, grounded in judgment, authorship, and purpose, and bounded by responsibility. Flow functions through a structured process, directing intellectual capital toward creativity within protective boundaries that preserve agency rather than replace it.

AI should be designed and implemented for a myriad of purposes: deploying the right knowledge at the right time to support investigation and exploration, enabling discovery for creative and research purposes, enhancing productivity and improving effectiveness, and enforcing governance structures for AI use. Boundaries ensure that patent rights and consent are respected; skilled humans control judgments, audits, and appeals; discovery does not stray into unproductive use of capital; and compliance with ethics and governance standards is maintained.

AI-generated outputs can be illuminating and, at times, transformative, but they are also fallible. This is where boundaries become essential. Effective use of AI to support creativity and innovation requires sufficient human capital and domain expertise to recognize errors, misdirection, or superficial plausibility. Verification and validation are not optional. AI-assisted insights must be tested, confirmed, and reconfirmed before they are integrated into creative or decision-making processes. When boundaries are well structured, human, structural, and ethical capital operate as checks on intellectual capital.

Organizations learn most effectively by deliberately designing capital and aligning AI use, revealing where value is created and where gaps persist. Capital budgeting exercises provide the practical setting in which boundaries generate feedback, making visible both strengths and strains within the capital system.

AI AS INNOVATION AMPLIFIER

While creativity concerns generating ideas, sounds, images, meanings, and possibilities, innovation concerns what happens next. Innovation is the disciplined process by which new ideas are translated into practices, products, systems, and services that create value in the real world. Joseph Schumpeter (1980) described innovation as a new combination of resources that disrupts existing arrangements and produces change in markets, institutions, and culture. Peter Drucker (2006) emphasized that innovation is purposeful and systematic, grounded in observation, opportunity recognition, and intentional design rather than in inspiration alone.

Innovation relies on creativity but extends beyond it. Creativity imagines what could be. Innovation tests, adapts, distributes, and sustains what works. In organizational settings, innovation requires feedback loops, structures for experimentation, tolerance for failure with clear limits, and moral clarity about who benefits and who bears the cost (Tidd and Bessant 2020).

AI can amplify innovation by accelerating experimentation, modeling scenarios, analyzing patterns across vast datasets, and reducing the time between idea and prototype. AI helps organizations spot emerging trends earlier, simulate outcomes before committing resources, and coordinate complex systems more effectively. Yet, AI does not eliminate human responsibility in innovation. Leaders must still assess and set risk boundaries, consider unintended consequences, evaluate ethical impacts, and decide when not to proceed.

AI is a catalyst for innovation, but conscience, wisdom, and governance structures remain the true authors of whether innovation promotes flourishing or accelerates disruption. By following the same precautions when using AI for creative purposes and by assessing risks with key stakeholders in the innovation process, boundaries are established, capital is well structured, and value creation is sustained.

AI PRODUCTIVITY: BENEFITS AND TRADE-OFFS

Productivity must always be interpreted, not merely measured. AI often delivers visible gains: tasks accelerate, reports finalize faster, and scheduling and analysis become easier to manage. Costs and redundancies can be reduced, and final output quality can be improved. These outcomes matter. Yet, productivity becomes ethically thin when treated as an end rather than a tool in the service of stakeholders, mission, human flourishing, and the common good. Markets generate value when participation is mutual rather than extractive. When one stakeholder gains only by diminishing another, markets drift toward zero-sum dynamics, ultimately weakening the very communities that sustain them.

Contemporary empirical research increasingly shows that firms that align their operations with broader ethical frameworks, reflected in Environmental, Social, and Governance and Corporate Social Responsibility activities, and with the United Nations Sustainable Development Goals tend to achieve stronger long-term financial performance, improved risk management, and more resilient value creation. Meta-analyses and longitudinal studies consistently identify positive relationships between sustainability practices and economic returns, with the strongest effects observed when such practices are material, strategic, and transparent (Friede, Busch, and Bassen 2015; Eccles, Ioannou, and Serafeim 2014; Khan, Serafeim, and Yoon 2016). Establishing and maintaining ethical boundaries in the pursuit of social and organizational productivity balances efficiency with well-being and returns.

History shows that technological acceleration can hollow out human capability when purpose is neglected. A physician who completes documentation faster but lacks emotional presence with patients is not more productive in any meaningful sense. A teacher who automates feedback may achieve grading efficiency while losing the formative encounter that shapes conscience and thinking. Speed alone is not productivity. Speed of operations or the loss of relational value can result in organizational confusion, employee turnover, and stakeholder withdrawal. Without direction, acceleration erodes human capital rather than cultivating it (Topol 2019; Acemoglu and Restrepo 2019).

Wise leaders understand that productivity is a conditional good. It must not merely balance the six forms of capital; it must strengthen them for the future. When efficiency frees time for presence, mentoring, reflection, and service, productivity forms people. When it accelerates output while diminishing humanity, it becomes extraction disguised as improvement. Prudence requires the discipline to see both benefits and trade-offs and to budget capital accordingly before consequences become irreversible. With proper understanding and boundaries, creativity, innovation, and productivity improve the top line, bottom line, and everything in between in social and organizational settings.

AI CAPITAL BUDGETING: SEEING CONSEQUENCES BEFORE THEY ARRIVE

AI is never merely about acquiring a new technology tool. It is a reallocation of capital. Deploying AI invariably reshapes human capital, intellectual systems, governance structures, finances, facilities, and culture. The implementation question shifts from *Can we afford this system?* to *What is the full range of impacts on the organization from using AI?* The answer to this critical question lies in capital budgeting.

Expanding capital budgeting tools to assess all forms of capital, with a disciplined assessment of short-, mid-, and long-term impacts, provides an excellent framework for analyzing the effects of implementing AI. Capital budgeting should be both qualitative and quantitative. Quantitative methods should employ established capital budgeting methods (Brealey et al. 2025). Thomas Copeland and Vladimir Antikarov (2001) show how real options methods can be used to develop flexibility, stage decisions, and reduce uncertainty. Real options methods also apply to AI deployment.

Qualitative or normative assessments help assess the deeper costs or benefits that often unfold more slowly. Human deskilling, dependence, weakened mentoring, institutional fragility, loss of institutional knowledge, and loss of trust develop gradually. Qualitative assessments personalize the effects of implementing new technology. Responsible leadership practices capital budgeting across short-, mid-, and long-term horizons to determine trade-offs and set limits to preserve and enhance capital (Brynjolfsson and McAfee 2016; Manyika et al. 2017).

A comprehensive capital budgeting exercise, with full stakeholder participation, may reveal that AI implementation may require significant investment in redeveloping human capital and in adjusting the mix of human capital within the organization. Awareness of the full impacts through disciplined budgeting is critical.

Tables 5.1–5.4 present a unique scenario. The scenarios illustrate how AI decisions may affect capital trajectories over time through the lens of the six capitals.

Capital budgeting represents a moral, visionary, and capital-awareness statement. It involves both qualitative and quantitative analyses, serving as a boundary and strategy-defining activity that promotes stakeholder engagement. Organizations that invest only in technology for cost savings and productivity may unintentionally neglect people, relationships, transparency, and culture. Conversely, by intentionally budgeting across all six forms of capital, AI can become a tool that develops organizational capital instead of simply replacing it.

TABLE 5.1   Scenario 1: Streamlining Administration and Reducing Staff

Capital	Short Term	Mid Term	Long Term
Human	Less paperwork, temporary relief	Skill loss, anxiety over job security	Weak leadership pipelines, burnout
Intellectual	Better record-keeping	Knowledge captured but shallow	Overreliance on automated systems
Structural	Faster workflows	Decisions follow automated defaults	Confusion during a disruption or an event failure
Financial	Visible savings	Rising vendor costs and integration	Turnover, retraining, and legal exposure
Physical	Smaller footprint	Systems optimized for automation	Difficult and costly to reverse if challenges arise
Ethical	Perception of modernization	Trust erosion as roles disappear	Loyalty loss, mission called into question, loss of tacit knowledge

Note: Intent: increase efficiency, reduce costs, simplify routines.
Prudent decision: proceed only with retraining pathways, role redesign, and explicit commitments to human formation; otherwise, savings quietly erode long-term resilience. Workforce redesign and new recruitment may mitigate savings. These qualitative scenarios can be run under different assumptions, supported by quantitative estimates.

TABLE 5.2   Scenario 2: Augmenting Rather Than Replacing Professionals

Capital	Short Term	Mid Term	Long Term
Human	Time returned for presence and mentoring	Skill deepening through guided practice	Strong vocational identity and leadership development
Intellectual	Knowledge organized and retrievable	Shared learning culture	Continuous improvement and disciplined innovation
Structural	Clear review processes	Transparent decision boundaries	Adaptable governance
Financial	Initial investment	Stable returns from quality gains	Sustainable value and reduced attrition
Physical	Better-aligned tools and workflows	Safer, more ergonomic environments	Resilient infrastructure
Ethical	Trust grows	Accountability remains visible	Institutional legitimacy strengthens

Note: Intent: improve quality, deepen expertise, and support judgment.
Prudent decision: invest first in training, governance, and human resources. Require AI to free up time for human work that only humans can do. Note that the work and skill redesign may allow attrition from old roles over time. The organization is harmonized in this scenario.

TABLE 5.3   Scenario 3: Writing Support Across a University

Capital	Short Term	Mid Term	Long Term
Human	Students complete assignments faster	Decline in analytical effort and revision habits	Loss of depth, dependent thinking, reduced originality
Intellectual	More polished submissions	Weak citation discipline emerges	Erosion of research literacy
Structural	Streamlined grading	Policy inconsistencies across courses	Academic integrity and achieved outcomes become ambiguous
Financial	Savings in instructional time	Increased oversight and misconduct cases	Reputational harm affects enrollment
Physical	Tech-enabled classrooms	Dependence on proprietary tools	Expensive renewal cycles
Ethical	Confusion about authorship	Quiet normalization of undisclosed assistance	Trust between faculty, students, and society erodes

Note: Intent: help students draft faster and reduce grading burdens without investing in additional mentoring or instructional staff.
Prudent decision: require transparency, attribution, staged training, and assignments that emphasize reasoning and reflection rather than output alone (Noy and Zhang 2023; US Copyright Office, Library of Congress 2023). The quality of writing and associated skill development can improve through intentional instruction in the writing process and the use of AI to support writing in staged, mentored activities.

TABLE 5.4   Scenario 4: Healthcare Documentation and Decision Support

Capital	Short Term	Mid Term	Long Term
Human	Reduced clerical burden	Better patient presence	Clinicians retain energy and focus on full vocational development activities
Intellectual	Organized histories	Pattern recognition improves	Safer clinical learning environments
Structural	Clear review workflows	Audit trails and oversight	Adaptive safety governance
Financial	Improved billing accuracy	Fewer burnout-related departures	Higher-quality care at lower downstream cost
Physical	Reduction in physical assets	Improved workflow design	Sustainable care environments
Ethical	Transparency improves	Shared accountability	Trust and timing of results between patients and clinicians grow

Note: Intent: reduce after-hours charting and improve diagnostic support.
Risks occur when clinicians uncritically rely on the system or when organizations see AI mainly as a way to boost volume (Samraik 2025; Topol 2019). A wise approach is to use AI as a support tool for decision-making and clinical documentation, not as the final authority. This should be combined with proper training, ongoing monitoring, institutional policies, and ethics review.

AI, like technology, transforms the capital mix, cost structures, and reliance networks. When implemented thoughtfully with clear boundaries and proper budgeting, AI can generate capital and promote the growth of humans, organizations, and society.

TAKEAWAYS

- Structural capital governs AI outcomes. Without clear rules, roles, accountability, and boundaries, AI adoption creates structural anarchy rather than value.

- Boundaries enable creativity and innovation. Proper limits do not restrict progress; they pace it so that ethics, formation, and institutions can keep pace with capability.

- Creativity is human; flow is structured. AI can support creative flow by reducing distractions and expanding access to knowledge, yet authorship and judgment remain human.

- Innovation requires governance. Translating ideas into value depends on feedback loops, experimentation, stakeholder engagement, and moral clarity.

- Productivity is a conditional good—speed and efficiency matter only when they strengthen capital, relationships, trust, and lasting outcomes.

- Every AI decision reallocates capital. Human, intellectual, structural, financial, physical, and ethical capital are always affected, often unevenly over time.

- Capital budgeting is foresight into value. Evaluating AI across short-, mid-, and long-term horizons reveals hidden trade-offs and prevents irreversible harm.

- Human capital comes first. If AI weakens judgment, mentoring, presence, or vocation, the investment is premature, regardless of apparent efficiency gains.

- Governance should be linked to ethical considerations and the shaping of capital.

NOTES

1 Langdon Winner, "Do Artifacts Have Politics?" *Daedalus* 109, no. 1 (1980): 121–136. Winner argues that technologies are not neutral instruments but often embody forms of power, privilege, and control that shape social behavior and political relationships as much as they improve efficiency. Through comparative examples of technical systems, he shows that design choices can either expand human freedom and participation or concentrate authority and dependency. His work invites careful discernment about the moral and political worlds that technologies quietly construct around their users.

2 Jacques Ellul, *The Technological Society*, trans. John Wilkinson (New York: Knopf, 1964). Ellul argues that modern technology, which he terms *technique*, is not merely a collection of tools but a self-reinforcing system that organizes society around efficiency, control, and predictability. In his account, technique tends toward autonomy, gradually subordinating human purpose, moral judgment, and freedom to its own internal logic. Rather than serving human flourishing, societies risk becoming servants of the systems they create. Ellul's warning highlights that the central question is never simply what technology can do, but what kind of world it quietly requires humans to inhabit.

WORKS CITED

Acemoglu, Daron, and Pascual Restrepo. 2019. "Automation and New Tasks: How Technology Displaces and Reinstates Labor." *Journal of Economic Perspectives* 33 (2): 3–30.

Amabile, Teresa M. 1996. *Creativity in Context: Update to the Social Psychology of Creativity*. Boulder, CO: Westview Press.

Brealey, Richard A., Stewart C. Myers, Franklin Allen, and Alex Edmans. 2025. *Principles of Corporate Finance*. New York: McGraw Hill.

Brynjolfsson, Erik, and Andrew McAfee. 2016. *The Second Machine Age: Work, Progress, and Prosperity in a Time of Brilliant Technologies*. New York: W. W. Norton & Company.

Copeland, Thomas E., and Vladimir Antikarov. 2001. *Real Options: A Practitioner's Guide*. New York: Texere.

Csikszentmihalyi, Mihaly. 1996. *Creativity: Flow and the Psychology of Discovery and Invention*. New York: HarperCollins.

Drucker, Peter F. 2006. *Innovation and Entrepreneurship*. New York: Harper Business.

Eccles, Robert G., Ioannis Ioannou, and George Serafeim. 2014. "The Impact of Corporate Sustainability on Organizational Processes and Performance." *Management Science* 60 (11): 2835–2857.

Ellul, Jacques. 1964. *The Technological Society*. Translated by John Wilkinson. New York: Vintage Books.

European Union. 2024, August 2. "Artificial Intelligence Act." *artificialintelligence-act.edu*. Accessed December 28, 2025. https://artificialintelligenceact.eu/ai-act-explorer

Europol. 2024, March 13. "Facing Reality Law Enforcement and the Challenge of Deepfakes, An Observatory Report from the Europol Innovation Lab." *Europol*. Publications Office of the European Union. Accessed December 28, 2025. https://www.europol.europa.eu/publications-events/publications/facing-reality-law-enforcement-and-challenge-of-deepfakes

Floridi, Luciano, and Massimo Chiriatti. 2020. "GPT-3: Its Nature, Scope Limits, and Consequences." *Minds and Machines* 30 (2): 1–14.

Friede, Gunnar, Timo Busch, and Alexander Bassen. 2015. "ESG and Financial Performance: Aggregated Evidence from More Than 2000 Empirical Studies." *Journal of Sustainable Finance & Investment* 5 (4): 210–233.

Heim, Lennart, Markus Anderljung, and Haydn Belfield. 2024, March 28. "To Govern AI, We Must Govern Compute." *Lawfare*. The Lawfare Institute in Cooperation with Brookings. Accessed December 28, 2025. https://www.lawfaremedia.org/article/to-govern-ai-we-must-govern-compute

Jonas, Hans. 1985. *The Imperative of Responsibility: In Search of an Ethics for the Technological Age*. Chicago: University of Chicago Press.

Khan, Mozaffar, George Serafeim, and Aaron Yoon. 2016. "Corporate Sustainability: First Evidence on Materiality." *Accounting Review* 91 (6): 1697–1724.

Manyika, James, Michael Chui, Mehdi Miremadi, Jacques Bughin, Katy George, Paul Willmott, and Martin Dewhurst. 2017, January. "A Future That Works: Automation, Employment, and Productivity." *McKinsey*. McKinsey Global Institute. Accessed December 29, 2025. https://www.mckinsey.com/~/media/mckinsey/featured%20insights/digital%20disruption/harnessing%20automation%20for%20a%20future%20that%20works/mgi-a-future-that-works-full-report-updated.pdf

North, Douglass C. 1990. *Institutions, Institutional Change and Economic Performance.* Cambridge, UK: Cambridge University Press.

Noy, Shakked, and Whitney Zhang. 2023. "Experimental Evidence on the Productivity Effects of Generative Artificial Intelligence." *Science* 381 (6654): 187–192.

O'Neil, Cathy. 2016. *Weapons of Math Destruction: How Big Data Increases Inequality and Threatens Democracy.* New York: Crown.

Pilati, Federico, and Tommaso Venturini. 2025. "The Use of Artificial Intelligence in Counter-Disinformation: A World Wide (Web) Mapping." *Frontiers in Political Science* 7. doi: 10.3389/fpos.2025.1517726

Roos, Goran, and Johan Roos. 1997. "Measuring Your Company's Intellectual Performance." *Long Range Planning* 30 (3): 413–426.

Russell, Stuart, and Peter Norvig. 2021. *Artificial Intelligence: A Modern Approach* (4th ed.). London, UK: Pearson.

Samraik, Mahima. 2025, October 17. "AI Scribes Reduce Physician Burnout and Return Focus to the Patient." *Yale School of Medicine.* Accessed December 29, 2025. https://medicine.yale.edu/news-article/ai-scribes-reduce-physician-burnout-return-focus-to-the-patient

Sawyer, R. Keith. 2012. *Explaining Creativity: The Science of Human Innovation.* Oxford: Oxford University Press.

Schumpeter, Joseph A. 1980. *The Theory of Economic Development.* New Brunswick: Routledge.

Sternberg, Robert J. 1988. "A Three-Facet Model of Creativity." In *The Nature of Creativity: Contemporary Psychological Perspectives*, edited by Robert J. Sternberg, 125–147. Cambridge: Cambridge University Press.

Stewart, Thomas A. 1997. *Intellectual Capital: The New Wealth of Organizations.* New York: Currency.

Throsby, David. 2001. *Economics and Culture.* Cambridge, UK: Cambridge University Press.

Tidd, Joe, and John R. Bessant. 2020. *Managing Innovation: Integrating Technological, Market and Organizational Change* (7th ed.). Hoboken: Wiley.

Topol, Eric. 2019. *Deep Medicine: How Artificial Intelligence Can Make Healthcare Human Again.* New York: Basic Books.

Tufekci, Zeynep. 2015. "Algorithmic Harms Beyond Facebook and Google: Emergent Challenges of Computational Agency." *Colorado Technology Law Journal* 13 (2): 203–217.

US Copyright Office, Library of Congress. 2023, March 16. "Copyright Registration Guidance: Works Containing Material Generated by Artificial Intelligence." *Federal Register.* Accessed December 29, 2025. https://www.federalregister.gov/documents/2023/03/16/2023-05321/copyright-registration-guidance-works-containing-material-generated-by-artificial-intelligence

Winner, Langdon. 1980. "Do Artifacts Have Politics?" *Daedalus* 109 (1): 121–136.

CHAPTER 6

Where Mission Meets Machine

AI in Education, Government Services, and NGOs

DEFINING PRODUCTIVITY IN MISSION-DRIVEN INSTITUTIONS

Mission-driven organizations define effectiveness differently from market-driven organizations. Their purpose is not primarily to maximize scale, throughput, or financial return, but to serve people, steward shared resources, and advance a clearly articulated social purpose. Trust, legitimacy, and human formation are not byproducts of mission-driven work; they are its core outcomes.

This difference in purpose shapes how efficiency, capital, and performance are understood. Efficiency is a means in mission-driven institutions, never an end. It exists to amplify mission, not replace it. Administrative clarity, reliable coordination, and prudent capital use enable organizations to serve people, care for the vulnerable, and remain accountable over time. When efficiency is pursued without reference to purpose, mission erodes. Efficiency means focusing the right capital on the right mission need at the right time.

Mission-driven work centers on people, the planet, and purpose. For many mission-rooted organizations, dignity is fundamental. People are seen not merely as units of output but as individuals with dignity, needs, and agency. The earth is not merely an externality; it is a shared inheritance that calls for responsible stewardship. Purpose provides guidance, discipline, and legitimacy, helping steer decisions, especially when resources are

DOI: 10.1201/9781003744061-6

limited. These principles collectively shape the unique identity of mission-driven organizations and their roles in stewardship and productivity.

Artificial intelligence (AI) serves in this environment as a powerful but constrained form of intellectual capital. When governed well, it helps mission-driven organizations clarify needs, coordinate services, reduce administrative burden, and free up time for human presence, accompaniment, mission-focused leadership, and personalized care. It improves consistency and access without displacing responsibility or relationships. Used poorly, it accelerates activity while weakening trust, obscuring accountability, and narrowing the mission to what can be easily measured.

Productivity in mission-driven organizations must be understood as service to people, stewardship of the planet, and fidelity to a mission-based purpose of service. Technology is legitimate only when it deepens care, strengthens responsibility, and reinforces dignity rather than substituting speed or scale for judgment and presence. When technology improves responsiveness, access, and understanding, it serves a mission-dependent purpose.

SIDEBAR 6.1   CONTRASTING MISSION-DRIVEN AND PROFIT-DRIVEN ORGANIZATIONS

Purpose and Needs

- Mission-driven organizations exist to meet human needs and those of the natural world that markets cannot fully address. These needs are often complex, relational, and context specific, requiring judgment, presence, and long-term accompaniment.
- Profit-driven organizations exist to meet market needs and wants that are sufficiently well defined and generalizable to support pricing, exchange, and competition.

Human Capital

- Mission-driven organizations rely on human capital, expressed through judgment, discretion, ethical responsibility, and relational presence, to interpret needs and sustain trust.
- Profit-driven organizations rely on human capital, expressed through expertise, innovation, and execution, to design, operate, and improve systems that meet market demand while maintaining stakeholder trust.

Capital Alignment

- Mission-driven organizations align capital to support and protect frontline human judgment where needs cannot be fully specified in advance.
- Profit-driven organizations align and grow capital to scale the productive, creative, and innovative capacity of human capital, leveraging standardization, automation, and market feedback.

AI and Human Capital

- In mission-driven organizations, AI serves as a constrained intellectual resource, aligned with structural and ethical capital that supports human capital by reducing administrative burden, improving access, and preserving space for judgment, presence, accompaniment, and accountability.
- In profit-driven organizations, AI amplifies human capital's ability to meet organizational goals and market-driven stakeholder needs, scaling expertise and coordination toward market-defined outcomes.

Risk and Failure

- Mission-driven organizations face asymmetric risk. Failures degrade human, ethical, and structural capital simultaneously, eroding trust and legitimacy, which are slow to rebuild.
- Profit-driven organizations face risks that are often first addressed through market responses and structural reconfiguration. Yet, repeated failures expose weaknesses in human judgment, ethical restraint, and governance, and markets signal whether to reform or reject.

Implications for AI Use

- In mission-driven organizations, AI must support work without displacing human presence, responsibility, or accountability. AI must be trained to distinguish between mission-driven and profit-driven data through refined algorithmic configurations.
- In profit-driven organizations, AI can be positioned closer to core operations, provided human accountability, ethical constraints, and governance remain in place.

In practice, there can be overlap between profit-driven organizations with high service applications and mission-oriented organizations.

These differences in purpose and capital alignment have direct implications for how AI systems are designed, trained, and governed in mission-driven organizations. AI that serves mission-driven work cannot be repurposed from profit-driven environments. It must be trained on data that reflect relational outcomes, contextual judgment, and long-term human impact rather than on transactional optimization alone. This customization requires deliberate curation of training data, explicit weighting of qualitative and longitudinal indicators, and algorithmic configurations that emphasize transparency, explainability, and human review over speed or scale.

In mission-driven contexts, AI must learn to surface needs, patterns, and risks without reducing persons to categories or outcomes to metrics. The effectiveness of AI in these settings depends not only on what it can predict but also on how it has been taught to respect, what it has been trained to ignore, and how its outputs remain subordinate to human judgment and responsibility.

EDUCATION: FORMATION THAT GUIDES AI USE

Education is a mission-driven institution whose purpose is human formation. It shapes attention, character, judgment, and belonging not merely by transmitting information but by the conditions in which learning occurs. Learning unfolds through relationships, repetition, presence, and struggle that lead to growth, correction, and encouragement. Instruction matters, but instruction detached from formation becomes technique without insight. Formation is the staged shaping of people as they grow in capability, responsibility, and understanding.

This relational account of learning reflects Lev Vygotsky's central insight: human learning is first social, then internal, and always mediated by relationships that scaffold growth (Vygotsky 1978).[1] Tools matter, but they operate within a psychosocial environment shaped by adults, peers, and norms. Because tools shape cognition, memory, language, and method, AI must support rather than displace the relational context in which learning and character develop.

Primary Education: Attention, Wonder, and Belonging

Primary education addresses human needs that markets and machines cannot adequately meet. Early childhood learning involves attention, attachment, conscience, trust, and belonging; capacities that are difficult to specify, price, or standardize. Piaget describes how children organize thought through symbolic play, imitation, stories, and hands-on exploration (Piaget 1974). Kohlberg shows that moral imagination develops through lived experiences of fairness, authority, consequences, and empathy rather than through abstract instruction alone (Kohlberg 1981). Economic research reaches a parallel conclusion using different methods: investments in early, relational, and just formation yield the highest lifelong returns (Psacharopoulos and Patrinos 2018; Heckman 2006).

AI supports education only to the extent that it strengthens formation. Adaptive tools, speech and language supports, and accessibility technologies can increase participation and reduce the administrative burden on teachers and mentors. When specifically trained, AI enables coordinated communication among teachers, families, and schools, freeing time for observation, listening, guidance, and care. Used in this way, AI strengthens human capital rather than displacing it. During this early formative period, AI use must be guided by teachers and parents through tools that scaffold discovery, remain self-contained, and limit data intrusion. AI training, algorithms, and data should be tailored to the needs of primary education.

In practice, this means treating AI in primary education as a curated, scaffolded library of approved tools rather than as unrestricted access to information. Such discipline preserves the formative purpose of education by ensuring that tools support learning goals rather than overwhelm developing judgment. Parents should be included to maintain continuity between school and home and to reinforce shared norms.

Primary students benefit from access to intellectual capital and early AI literacy. Still, responsibility for alignment rests with educators, administrators, and parents or guardians, who govern use through ethical and structural frameworks that cultivate age-appropriate judgment and ethical capacity (Livingstone and Blum-Ross 2020).

Primary Learning and AI Applications

Effective AI use in primary classrooms supports the quiet work of formation and the teacher. Consider a classroom that uses adaptive reading software to identify phonics gaps and suggest targeted practice. The teacher remains the interpreter: listening, reassuring, and preventing frustration from hardening into shame. The instructional rhythm remains human: demonstration, shared practice, individual effort, and revision. Feedback to students, offered within a trusting relationship and supported by technology, strengthens motivation, comprehension, and endurance (Hattie and Timperley 2007).

In this arrangement, AI identifies patterns while teachers cultivate confidence, perseverance, and a sense of meaning. Technology supports language development, vocabulary scaffolding, and decoding skills, while educators frame understanding and protect dignity. AI excels at helping teachers detect early learning challenges and tailor follow-up, freeing time for reading aloud, conversation, and guided discovery – practices essential to early literacy development (National Reading Panel 2000; Fillmore and Snow 2018).

The same approach applies to mathematics. When technology demonstrates mathematical logic and helps students see mathematics as connected to the real world rather than as just abstract concepts, they start to view it as a problem-solving language, which boosts their numeracy and confidence (Boaler 2022).

Character development occurs through storytelling, modeling, and group discussions. While digital prompts and visual aids are helpful, teachers and families play a crucial role in demonstrating and promoting ethical use. Schools that incorporate adaptive tools alongside guided reading circles, peer dialogue, and teacher coaching see improvements in fluency while maintaining a sense of belonging and community (Pane et al. 2017). When AI serves as a supportive aide rather than a judge, students tend to persevere longer and are less likely to internalize failure.

The risks are equally evident. Understaffing or budget constraints might lead to the use of automated assessment tools that simplify learning into dashboards, produce scores without providing meaningful feedback, and quietly classify students. Teachers may feel compelled to teach to the algorithm, while students may start to see themselves as labels rather than active learners. Although instruction speeds up, depth and personal development diminish, and technology begins influencing identity in ways that undermine dignity and trust.

Access to social media during primary school years is a major concern. Many AI-powered social media platforms prioritize maximizing user engagement over promoting character building or personal growth (Livingstone and Blum-Ross 2020; Twenge 2018). As screens become more pervasive, opportunities for meaningful conversations, creative pursuits, and character development decline.

Primary school leaders and teachers are integral to the capital architecture ecosystem. Capital encompasses more than just human capital or mission components; it includes the leverage tools that support and enhance it.

SIDEBAR 6.2   SIX-CAPITAL IMPACTS IN PRIMARY EDUCATION

Human Capital

Attention, curiosity, trust, moral imagination, perseverance, and belonging are shaped by relationships with teachers, families, and peers.

Ethical Capital

Norms of dignity, fairness, patience, and care that govern how children are assessed, corrected, encouraged, and protected from premature labeling or shame.

Intellectual Capital

Curricula, pedagogical knowledge, behavioral, literacy, and numeracy frameworks, and AI tools that support diagnosis, scaffolding, and understanding without replacing judgment.

Structural Capital

School routines, classroom practices, communication pathways, governance policies, and accountability structures that protect formation and guide responsible AI use.

Financial Capital

Resources allocated to teacher development, learning materials, support services, and technology that serve formation rather than efficiency alone.

Physical Capital

Classroom spaces, books, learning materials, and technological infrastructure that support attention, safety, and shared learning.

Capital Hierarchy Insight

In primary education, ethical and human capital govern the use of intellectual and structural capital. AI strengthens education only when it is subordinate to formation, guided by ethical purpose, and embedded in relational practice.

Primary education lays the foundation for attention, trust, language, numeracy, literacy, social exploration, natural curiosity, and moral imagination through guided development and relational presence. As children grow, the focus of education evolves. Human capital broadens in scope and complexity as adolescents develop abstract reasoning, self-awareness, agency, and responsibility. Learning shifts from acquiring fundamental skills to shaping judgment, identity, and intellectual authorship, all in preparation for independence, work, and vocation.

During adolescence, AI remains a form of intellectual capital, but the associated risks and opportunities shift. Tools that once supported discovery must now be managed to promote discernment, accountability, and self-regulation. The challenge at the secondary level is not only whether AI can aid learning but also whether it enhances or undermines young people's emerging abilities to think critically, make choices, and act responsibly.

SECONDARY EDUCATION: FORMATION FOR FREEDOM, WORK, AND VOCATION

Secondary education unfolds on a different developmental horizon from primary schooling. As foundational skills take root, adolescents confront questions of identity, belonging, conscience, and responsibility. Students' cognitive capacity expands, their abstract reasoning strengthens, and peer influence intensifies (Steinberg 2015). At this stage, education is no longer primarily about acquiring skills but about cultivating intellectual abilities, discerning a vocation, and developing the capacity to make responsible choices.

AI can assist with research, tutoring, organizing writing, and providing quick feedback. However, it may also promote shortcuts, delegate thinking, and heighten comparison and performance anxiety. Because adolescents are still maturing neurologically, particularly in impulse control, foresight, and risk assessment, AI doesn't eliminate developmental challenges (Casey, Getz, and Galvan 2008). Instead, it can support students' ongoing learning or hinder it by enabling superficial imitation. During this stage, deliberate mentoring and clear boundaries are essential to ensure that these tools reinforce, rather than weaken, the development of sound judgment.

Teachers play a decisive role in this process. They guide students not only in what to know but also in how to evaluate evidence, question assumptions, and uphold integrity. Secondary education becomes an apprenticeship in accepting accountability, discerning ideas, assessing how they fit in the world, and evaluating knowledge. Ideas carry moral weight, and habits of the mind are shaped during this phase. As in primary education, AI tools should be trained, algorithms fine-tuned, and data use categorized for age-appropriate secondary education, where scaffolded exploration and the introduction to philosophical ideas need to be grounded in the world and shaped through explanation. AI use is part manicured AI application and part guided use of open-access AI tools.

Secondary Classroom and AI Applications

Consider a class that prepares students to write analytical essays. Students develop ideas, articulate a thesis, and create an outline. With faculty guidance and parental awareness, they use AI tools to organize notes, refine outlines, and summarize research sources. Students are explicitly taught to verify and validate AI-assisted outputs. Drafting, revision, oral defense, and critique remain human centered. Learning unfolds through effort, dialogue, feedback, and revision. Voice develops, and accountability remains clear. Guided AI use supports refinement rather than substitution, helping students recognize both the power and limits of technological assistance. Feedback that emphasizes reasoning rather than correctness strengthens motivation and competence (Nicol and Macfarlane-Dick 2006).

When used deliberately and with mentorship, AI can support discovery across disciplines without displacing student originality. In mathematics, students may explore alternative solution paths or visualize how changing assumptions affect the problem while remaining responsible for selecting methods, explaining their reasoning orally, and verifying their work through alternative competency-based assessments.

In science courses, AI can scaffold the iterative development of hypothesis generation and simulation, and help organize data analysis, while students design experiments, interpret evidence, and draw their own conclusions. Students learn methods, analysis, and discovery with support.

In social studies, AI may summarize primary sources, map historical trends, and explore counterfactual social possibilities, but students retain responsibility for evaluating credibility, identifying bias, and constructing arguments. In each case, AI expands the intellectual workspace available to students, while discovery and creativity remain human acts shaped by judgment, reflection, and ethical responsibility.

To reinforce accountability, students should maintain an AI-use journal that documents how they use tools for each assignment. This practice makes authorship visible and creates opportunities for guided reflection rather than dependence. Teachers can then help students distinguish between assistance and substitution and assess both academic growth and the responsible use of technology. When instruction on AI use is integrated across courses rather than confined to isolated modules, students develop consistent habits of ethical engagement. Disclosure, reflection, and guided practice reinforce discernment and responsibility over time.

Risk arises when AI shifts from tutor to author. Essays are generated rather than written, analytics sort students into static categories, and assessment becomes confused. AI can diminish when it facilitates an academic shift from mastery to short-term advancement. Overreliance on technology, including AI, may weaken metacognitive abilities and authentic skill development (Luckin et al. 2016). At this developmental stage, formation requires authentic academic authorship, responsibility, and learned pathways to inquiry. Shortcuts diminish life-defining abilities and habits, and habits shape futures.

Pathways to Work and Vocation

As students mature, their horizons widen. Many pursue apprenticeships, trade programs, technical education, employment, or tertiary education. These choices now carry lasting consequences. Education guides students toward pathways that integrate skill, meaning, stewardship, and service.

In vocational and technical programs, AI-enabled simulators and diagnostic systems support safe, repeatable practice. Nursing students triage virtual patients, automotive students interpret fault codes and then verify the results manually, and manufacturing students visualize complex systems before operation. Guided AI and AI-enabled tools accelerate competence without replacing human mentorship (Sawyer 2014).

AI also supports counseling and planning by mapping pathways, estimating costs, and highlighting labor-market trends. Properly used, these systems expand opportunity, particularly for first-generation students navigating unfamiliar terrain (Carnevale et al. 2018). Yet, AI models reflect assumptions and incomplete data. They can narrow horizons or suggest short-term outcomes at the expense of vocation, stewardship, and the common good. Discernment and the finalization of vocation remain human tasks. AI supplies information: mentors, families, and communities help interpret its meaning and direction.

Higher Education Preparation: Choosing With Wisdom, Not Strategy Alone

For students preparing for higher education, AI serves as a research and planning companion. It compares programs, models scenarios, and organizes information about institutional fit. Counselors slow the process, helping students frame questions about talents, limits, aspirations, well-being, and belonging. Students may use AI for structural feedback on personal statements, while teachers, parents, and peers safeguard authenticity through discussion and clarification (Yeager and Dweck 2012).

Next-level education exploration extends beyond rankings and admission strategies to include support, community, health care, costs, human capital returns, and realistic completion timelines. AI performs well at generating comparisons and scenarios. Human judgment remains essential for interpreting what constitutes a sound and sustainable fit. Evidence consistently shows that alignment among students, institutions, and support systems matters more than institutional prestige alone (Kuh et al. 2005).

Education leaders, teachers, and governing boards, working with parents, design and develop a highly diverse secondary school infrastructure. This system aims to support a diverse student population with varied needs, goals, and abilities.

SIDEBAR 6.3   SIX-CAPITAL IMPACTS IN SECONDARY EDUCATION

Human Capital

Judgment, authentic authorship, self-regulation, responsibility, identity formation, and the capacity to choose and act with integrity.

Ethical Capital

Norms governing honesty, authorship, accountability, fairness, and the moral aspects of intellectual work and vocational choice.

Intellectual Capital

Curricula, disciplinary knowledge, research methods, and AI tools that support inquiry, synthesis, and reflection without replacing thinking.

Structural Capital

Assessment practices, governance policies, mentoring systems, and AI-use frameworks that preserve transparency, authentic authorship, and accountability.

Financial Capital

Investments in counseling, vocational programs, simulations, support services, and learning technologies are crafted to foster long-term formation rather than short-term metrics.

Physical Capital

Workshops, laboratories, classrooms, digital infrastructure, and community spaces that support practice, collaboration, and supervised exploration.

Capital Hierarchy Insight

In secondary education, ethical and human capital guide the use of intellectual and structural capital. AI enhances learning by supporting students' original work, critical thinking, and career exploration. However, it weakens development when it replaces effort, judgment, or personal responsibility.

As students move toward tertiary education or the workforce, the locus of formation shifts again. Human capital is developed and exercised with greater autonomy, specialization, and accountability. Learning now involves advanced disciplinary mastery, professional identity, and sustained intellectual responsibility. AI remains intellectual capital, but its influence deepens as students engage with larger knowledge systems, research methods, and professional norms.

TERTIARY HIGHER EDUCATION: PROFESSION, JUDGMENT, AND RESPONSIBILITY

Tertiary higher education operates within a more diverse and complex landscape than earlier learning phases. It no longer adheres to a single institutional framework or a linear pathway. Instead, it comprises a network of venues and credentials designed to serve recent graduates, working adults, first-generation students, veterans, caregivers, apprentices, and those seeking reskilling. Learning occurs across residential universities, online and hybrid courses, community colleges, technical and trade schools, apprenticeships, internships, service-learning initiatives, and partnerships with employers and military organizations.

This diversity is a strength, as it reflects the reality that human capital develops unevenly over time and across contexts. However, public trust in higher education has declined, with families questioning costs, debt, ideology, and whether institutions still effectively prepare capable and ethical adults. Employers are now more focused on whether degrees genuinely indicate judgment, reliability, and responsibility (Brenan 2023). Currently, higher education faces vulnerabilities at the institutional level, and AI integration occurs within this fragile trust environment.

AI can significantly aid tertiary higher education by organizing knowledge, identifying gaps, and alleviating cognitive load. It supports brainstorming, outlining, feedback, and interdisciplinary inquiry. When used appropriately, AI serves as an intellectual aid and a support tool, akin to libraries, laboratories, tutors, and simulations. However, ethical boundaries are crossed if AI-generated work is submitted as original, if it replaces reasoning instead of encouraging it, or if false or unchecked sources are accepted as authoritative.

Sound AI use in tertiary higher education follows long-standing norms governing authorship, intellectual property, and verification. Shortcutting the developmental process was unacceptable before AI and remains so now. Institutions must adapt assessment and verification practices. Practical approaches include requiring notes and outlines, AI and technology-use disclosures, drafts and revision histories, oral defenses, in-class discussion, and comparison with a student's prior intellectual record (Bittle and El-Gayar 2025). These practices preserve authentic authorship while allowing AI to serve as intellectual capital.

Across institutional settings, AI's role varies, but its constraints remain consistent. In residential universities, AI may support inquiry and tutoring, but it cannot replace mentoring, dialogue, or the moral life of a learning community. In online and hybrid programs, AI can improve accessibility and personalization, but belonging and achievement remain relational. In competency-based programs, AI may reveal gaps in mastery, but it must not define mastery itself. In community colleges, AI can clarify pathways and advising for working adults while resisting profiling or narrowing opportunities.

In technical and trade programs, AI powers diagnostics and simulation, yet craft, safety, and mastery are developed through supervised practice. In apprenticeships and internships, AI may support reflection, but responsibility is learned through action, consequences, and accountability. Even accelerated pathways require restraint: AI may support preparation, but it should not compress the slow work of demonstration, discussion, and growth.

Practiced ethically, AI can deepen learning across disciplines. In the sciences, it supports simulation, data analysis, and visualization. In business, it assists with financial modeling and scenario planning without replacing prudent judgment. In medicine, it supports diagnostics and literature review while leaving care, consent, and responsibility in human hands. In engineering, it models designs and constraints, yet professionals must still understand physical limits and ethical consequences. In all cases, students must be able to explain, defend, and justify AI-assisted outputs to demonstrate mastery. Human development and professional responsibility remain the mission outcomes of tertiary education.

The risks of misuse are equally clear. Institutions increasingly rely on dashboards to monitor performance and behavior. When analytics replace dialogue, mass assessment replaces formative feedback, and systems go unchecked, students learn to comply rather than to judge and master. AI systems magnify harm because, when unchecked, they resist scrutiny and appeal to efficiency (O'Neil 2016). Dashboards support learning only when they are transparent, co-designed with faculty and students, and subordinate to human judgment.

The goal of tertiary higher education is not merely to maximize AI use but to cultivate adults who understand when AI assistance is appropriate and when it should be limited. AI represents a sophisticated form of intellectual capital, and its acceptance hinges on how institutions govern and utilize it. Faculty and administrators are progressively integrating AI into advising, assessment, research support, and course development. When these applications are transparent, appropriately limited, and aligned with pedagogical and ethical goals, they promote responsible and ethical use.

When the use of AI and related practices is unclear and focused only on efficiency, it undermines institutional credibility. It confuses students about who owns and is responsible for intellectual work. Higher education is successful when graduates understand the ethical use of intellectual property to make professional decisions, take on vocational responsibilities, and contribute positively to society. Ultimately, formation, the development of character and judgment, remains the key measure of success.

Building capital in a tertiary higher education context involves engaging stakeholders. Various interests intersect uniquely through research, scholarship, training, leadership, knowledge enhancement, and readiness for graduate studies.

SIDEBAR 6.4 SIX-CAPITAL IMPACTS IN TERTIARY HIGHER EDUCATION

Human Capital

Advanced judgment, professional identity, ethical responsibility, self-direction, and accountability for consequential decisions.

Ethical Capital

Norms governing authorship, intellectual honesty, professional responsibility, consent, and the moral consequences of expertise.

Intellectual Capital

Disciplinary knowledge, research methods, professional standards, and AI tools that support inquiry, synthesis, and modeling without replacing reasoning.

Structural Capital

Assessment regimes, accreditation standards, governance policies, AI-use rules, and verification practices that preserve transparency and accountability.

Financial Capital

Investments in instruction, mentoring, research infrastructure, student support, and learning technologies align with long-term formation rather than credentialing throughput.

Physical Capital

Laboratories, classrooms, workshops, clinics, digital platforms, and community spaces that support supervised practice, experimentation, and collaboration.

Capital Hierarchy Insight

In tertiary education, ethical and human capital govern the use of advanced intellectual and structural capital. AI strengthens professional formation when it supports judgment, verification, and responsibility. It erodes legitimacy when it substitutes for intellectual authorship, obscures accountability, or accelerates credentialing without formation.

PUBLIC SERVICE AND CIVIL SOCIETY: TRUST, JUSTICE, AND PRESENCE

Governmental and non-governmental organizations (NGOs) do not replace one another. They form a complementary, mission-driven ecosystem of moral responsibility. At their best, governments provide order, justice, and the common goods that markets alone cannot deliver. NGOs step in when institutional capacity strains, gaps widen, or people fall outside formal systems of care. Together, they shape how societies experience trust, fairness, and human dignity.

Government operates across multiple layers, including local, regional, national, and international systems. Each layer touches daily life through housing, transportation, policing, public health, disaster response, the courts, taxation, and environmental stewardship. When government acts justly and transparently, societies flourish. When it fails, harm escalates quickly and often disproportionately.

Across many nations, public trust in government and some NGOs has eroded. Citizens increasingly view public institutions as distant, complex, or unresponsive. Research shows that perceptions of unfairness and a lack of transparency erode legitimacy and civic participation (Levi and Stoker 2000). Global trust surveys reinforce this pattern, particularly when institutions deploy technologies that lack transparency, such as AI, without clear accountability (Edelman Trust Institute 2024).

When used effectively, AI can enhance public service and civil society. In accountable systems, AI helps minimize fraud, waste, and abuse, improves the precision of aid delivery, and strengthens oversight without replacing human judgment (OECD 2025). Local governments can leverage AI for tasks such as inspections, maintenance, emergency responses, translation, and improving service accessibility. At broader levels, regional and national, AI can identify anomalies in areas such as education, health, taxation, courts, transportation, and environmental risks that require human review and action. Governments also have a responsibility to regulate and establish both structural and ethical frameworks for AI use to prevent misuse.

When systems are integrated with blockchain-based ledgers, they can verify logistics chains and payment flows while ensuring auditability and transparency. Humanitarian organizations already use these tools to enhance traceability and transparency in aid delivery while upholding human governance and ethical standards (Dimitropoulos 2022; Dumitriu 2020; World Food Programme n.d.). The goal of using AI and related mission-driven technologies is not to exert control but to enhance institutional capacity to serve people with fairness, accuracy, and compassion.

AI plays a key role at both federal and international levels, aiding in coordinating benefits, disaster response, national security, climate monitoring, disease tracking, and humanitarian logistics. When well regulated, these systems prevent redundancy and enhance legitimate access. However, poor governance can lead to increased exclusion and errors, particularly when transparency and the ability to challenge decisions are lacking (Eubanks 2018). While blockchain can help maintain record integrity, it is still crucial to ensure due process, oversight, appeal rights, and correction mechanisms, as mistakes in these systems can cause significant harm.

NGOs encounter comparable challenges. AI can help organize volunteers, manage scheduling, translate languages, and detect needs. Blockchain can boost donor trust and enable resource distribution tracking. However, NGOs are not only about providing services but also about supporting individuals. Presence, attentive listening, and trustworthiness are still crucial. Technology should enhance relationships and care, not substitute for them (Ramiah n.d.).

A core guiding principle stays unchanged. In mission-focused settings, technology can improve transparency and verification processes. However, it should never act as a barrier that excludes people from services or eliminates mercy, the right to appeal, or the chance for correction. AI should be used in public service and civil society only if it promotes human well-being by ensuring access, fairness, accountability, and meaningful human involvement when it matters most.

SIDEBAR 6.5   SIX-CAPITAL IMPACTS IN PUBLIC SERVICE AND CIVIL SOCIETY

Human Capital

Judgment, discretion, presence, ethical capacity, and the ability to serve people fairly and humanely.

Ethical Capital

Norms of justice, transparency, due process, restraint, consent, and protection of the vulnerable.

Intellectual Capital

Policy knowledge, data analysis, insights into dignity, institutional memory, and AI tools that support insight without replacing judgment.

Structural Capital

Governance systems, accountability mechanisms, appeal processes, audit trails, and verification frameworks.

Financial Capital

Public funds, donor resources, and budgets are stewarded to reduce waste while expanding service and access.

Physical Capital

Facilities, infrastructure, equipment, and service environments designed to support presence, dignity, and accessibility.

Capital Hierarchy Insight

In public service and civil society, ethical and human capital govern the use of AI-enabled intellectual and structural capital. AI strengthens legitimacy when it clarifies responsibility and improves access. It erodes trust when it replaces judgment, obscures accountability, or silently excludes people.

MISSION-DRIVEN ETHICAL AI CHECKLIST

Mission Before Capability

Begin with purpose.

- ☐ Does AI use strengthen service to people rather than simply accelerating tasks?

- ☐ Does AI free up time for human presence, judgment, and care?

- ☐ Would specific actions still be chosen without AI?

- ☐ Could a specific use of AI weaken trust, dignity, or belonging?

If efficiency improves but human outcomes worsen, do not deploy.

Human Dignity and Ethical Capital

- ☐ Does any system rank, score, or sort people without human review?

- ☐ Is there a clear avenue for appeal, correction, and explanation?

- ☐ Are vulnerable populations protected?

If dignity is at risk, redesign.

Formation Before Automation

- ☐ Does AI clarify, coach, or support rather than replace effort?

- ☐ Can the student, client, or citizen explain the outcome or their needs in their own words?

- ☐ Is a teacher, counselor, social worker, or official still central?

Shortcuts erode judgment and character.

Six-Capital Stewardship

- ☐ Human capital is strengthened through learning, confidence, and agency.

- ☐ Intellectual capital is verified through sources, citations, validity, and review.

☐ Structural capital promotes transparency, contestability, and fairness.

☐ Financial capital reduces waste while expanding service.

☐ Physical capital supports safe, dignified, human-centered spaces.

☐ Ethical capital reflects justice, disclosure, restraint, and accountability.

Transparency, Consent, and Disclosure

☐ People are informed when AI is used to determine outcomes.

☐ Data sources and limitations are clearly disclosed.

☐ Privacy and consent are respected.

Accountability and Verification

☐ A named person owns decisions and explains them.

☐ Logs, audits, and appeals are active and reviewed by competent humans.

☐ No high-stake decision relies solely on AI.

Red-Light Indicators

☐ AI replaces judgment in consequential decisions.

☐ Outputs cannot be explained or challenged.

☐ People are silently excluded or categorized.

☐ Responsibility is obscured.

Green-Light Indicators

☐ More time for presence and service.

☐ Humans decide and verify.

☐ Trust and ethical capital increase.

Mission-driven institutions concentrate their efforts in a high-trust environment that prioritizes people and the planet. AI works most effectively when customized for these mission-focused contexts, improving service and maintaining integrity.

TAKEAWAYS

- Productivity in mission-driven institutions is moral, not about optimization. True mission-driven productivity strengthens people, trust, and capital over time. AI is justified only when it deepens presence, judgment, and service.

- Formation always precedes automation. Education, government, and civil society exist to form persons and safeguard justice. AI must support this work without replacing human presence, judgment, or responsibility.

- Trust is the real currency of mission-driven organizations. Organizations fail not primarily because of technological breakdown but because of moral failure. When trust erodes, all six forms of capital decay.

- AI is a scaffold, not a shortcut. Used well, it frees time for teaching, counseling, and service. Used poorly, AI shortcuts effort, original authorship, and accountability.

- Technology must never judge the human person. Systems that silently score or sort undermine dignity. Appeal, correction, and mercy must remain visible and tangible.

- Capital reveals whether AI serves the mission or consumes it. Where AI strengthens presence, fairness, and responsibility, capital grows. Where it replaces relationships or obscures accountability, decay sets in.

- Ethical governance is the frontier. Mission determines how AI is used. AI remains a tool for human flourishing.

NOTE

1 Lev S. Vygotsky, *The Development of Higher Psychological Processes* (Cambridge, MA: Harvard University Press, 1978), 7–9. Writing within a framework shaped by historical materialism, Vygotsky understood human development as embedded in social structures, material conditions, and cultural practices. Human consciousness emerges through tools, symbols, work, and communal life

rather than in isolation. In this view, intellectual, structural, and ethical capital interact to shape perception, behavior, and identity. Vygotsky emphasized that tools do not merely alter nature but also transform the humans who employ them. Contemporary technologies such as AI participate in this same dynamic by reshaping habits of mind, relationships, and the moral imagination.

WORKS CITED

Banks, Nicola, David Hulme, and Michael Edwards. 2015. "NGOs, States, and Donors Revisited: Still Too Close for Comfort." *World Development* 66: 707–718.

Bittle, Kyle, and Omar F. El-Gayar. 2025. "Generative AI and Academic Integrity in Higher Education: A Systematic Review and Research Agenda." *Information* 16 (4): 296.

Boaler, Jo. 2022. *Mathematical Mindsets: Unleashing Students' Potential Through Creative Mathematics, Inspiring Messages and Innovative Teaching* (2nd ed.). San Francisco: Jossey-Bass.

Brenan, Megan. 2023, July 11. "Americans' Confidence in Higher Education Down Sharply." *Gallup News*. Accessed January 1, 2026. https://news.gallup.com/poll/508352/americans-confidence-higher-education-down-sharply.aspx

Carnevale, Anthony P., Jeff Strohl, Neil Ridley, and Artem Gulish. 2018. *Three Educational Pathways to Good Jobs: High Schools, Middle Skills, and Bachelor's Degree*. Washington, DC: Georgetown University Center on Education and the Workforce.

Casey, B.J., Sarah J. Getz, and Adriana Galvan. 2008. "The Adolescent Brain." *Developmental Review* 28 (1): 62–77.

Columbia Law School. 2016, December 19. *Flint Water Crisis Investigation*. Sabin Center for Climate Change Law Columbia Law School. Accessed December 30, 2025. https://climate.law.columbia.edu/content/flint-water-crisis-investigation

Dimitropoulos, Georgios. 2022. "The Use of Blockchain by International Organizations: Effectiveness and Legitimacy." *Policy and Society* 41 (3): 328–342.

Dumitriu, Petru. 2020. *Blockchain Applications in the United Nations System: Toward a State of Readiness*. Accessed January 1, 2026. https://docs.un.org/en/JIU/REP/2020/7

Edelman Trust Institute. 2024. *Edelman Trust Barometer*. Accessed January 1, 2026. https://www.edelman.com/sites/g/files/aatuss191/files/2024-02/2024%20Edelman%20Trust%20Barometer%20Global%20Report_FINAL.pdf

Eubanks, Virginia. 2018. *Automating Inequality: How High-Tech Tools Profile, Police and Punish the Poor*. New York: St. Martin's Press.

Fillmore, Lily Wong, and Catherine E. Snow. 2018. "What Teachers Need to Know About Language." In *What Teachers Need to Know About Language*, edited by Carolyn Temple Adger, Catherine E. Snow, and Donna Christian, 8–51. Bristol: Multilingual Matters.

Hanushek, Eric A., Jacob D. Light, Paul E. Peterson, Laura M. Talpey, and Ludger Woessmann. 2020. "Long-Run Trends in the U.S. SES--Achievement Gap." *NBER Working Paper 26764*. Cambridge, MA: NBER.

Hattie, John, and Helen Timperley. 2007. "The Power of Feedback." *Review of Educational Research* 77 (1): 81–112.

Heckman, James. 2006. "Skill Formation and the Economics of Investing in Disadvantaged Children." *Science* 312 (5782): 1900–1902.

Kohlberg, Lawrence. 1981. *The Philosophy of Moral Development: Moral Stages and the Idea of Justice*, Vol. 1. Essays on Moral Development. San Francisco, CA: Harper & Row.

Kuh, George D., Jillian Kinzie, John H. Schuh, and Elizabeth J. Whitt. 2005. *Student Success in College: Creating Conditions That Matter*. San Francisco, CA: Jossey-Bass.

Levi, Margaret, and Laura Stoker. 2000. "Political Trust and Trustworthiness." *Annual Review of Political Science* 3 (1): 475–507.

Livingstone, Sonia, and Alicia Blum-Ross. 2020. *Parenting for a Digital Future: How Hopes and Fears About Technology Shape Children's Lives*. New York: Oxford University Press.

Luckin, Rosemary, Wayne Holmes, Mark Griffiths, and Laurie B. Forcier. 2016. *Intelligence Unleashed: An Argument for AI in Education*. London: Pearson.

Nicol, David J., and Debra Macfarlane-Dick. 2006. "Formative Assessment and Self-Regulated Learning: A Model and Seven Principles of Good Feedback Practice." *Studies in Higher Education* 31 (2): 199–218.

O'Neil, Cathy. 2016. *Weapons of Math Destruction: How Big Data Increases Inequality and Threatens Democracy*. New York: Crown.

OECD. 2025, September 18. *Governing with Artificial Intelligence: The State of Plan and Way Forward in Core Government Functions*. Accessed January 1, 2026. https://www.oecd.org/en/publications/2025/06/governing-with-artificial-intelligence_398fa287/full-report/ai-in-fighting-corruption-and-promoting-public-integrity_60f5c50a.html

Pane, John F., Elizabeth D. Steiner, Matthew Baird, and Laura S. Hamilton. 2017. *Informing Progress: Insights on Personalized Learning Implementation and Effects*. Santa Monica, CA: Rand Corporation.

Piaget, Jean. 1974. *Origins of Intelligence in Children*. New York: International Universities Press Inc.

Pondiscio, Robert. 2015, April 3. *Accountability on Trial: The Atlanta School Cheating Convictions Are Unhelpful to Education Reform*. Accessed December 30, 2025. https://www.usnews.com/opinion/knowledge-bank/2015/04/03/atlanta-school-cheating-convictions-unhelpful-for-education-reform

Psacharopoulos, George, and Harry A. Patrinos. 2018. *Returns to Investment in Education: A Decennial Review of the Global Literature*. Working Paper, World Bank Policy Research Working Paper No. 8402, Washington, DC: World Bank.

Ramiah, Devandand. n.d. *5 Ways AI Can Help Crisis Response Around the World*. Accessed January 1, 2026. https://www.undp.org/5-ways-ai-can-help-crisis-response-around-world

Report of the National Reading Panel. 2000. *Teaching Children to Read*. Washington, DC: U.S. Government Printing Office.

Sawyer, R. Keith. 2014. *The Cambridge Handbook of the Learning Sciences* (2nd ed.). New York: Cambridge University Press.

Steinberg, Laurence. 2015. *Age of Opportunity: Lessons from the New Science of Adolescence*. New York: Harper Paperbacks.

Twenge, Jean M. 2018. *iGen: Why Today's Super-Connected Kids Are Growing Up Less Rebellious, More Tolerant, Less Happy – and Completely Unprepared for Adulthood*. New York: Atria Books.

Vygotsky, Lev S. 1978. *Development of Higher Psychological Processes*. Cambridge, MA: Cambridge: Harvard University Press.

World Food Programme. n.d. *Building Blocks: Blockchain Network for Humanitarian Assistance*. Accessed January 1, 2026. https://innovation.wfp.org/project/building-blocks

Yeager, David Scott, and Carol S. Dweck. 2012. "Mindsets That Promote Resilience: When Students Believe That Personal Characteristics Can Be Developed." *Educational Psychologist* 47 (4): 302–314.

CHAPTER 7

Next-Generation Nets

From AI Misalignment to Capital-Driven Human Flourishing

TECHNOLOGICAL PROMISE TO GOVERNED CAPABILITY: THE HUMAN–AI GOAL

Technological advancement is not a goal but a pathway to human well-being, assessed by the ongoing enhancement of four key dignities: human dignity, the dignity of the natural environment, the dignity of space and place, and the dignity of free will and conscience. Dignity and cultivated progress are stepping stones to realizing well-being. Artificial intelligence (AI) must evolve into a form of intellectual capital that promotes growth aligned with human values. Historically, new tools have been significant not merely because of their novelty or power but because they changed the conditions under which humans learn, work, govern, and thrive. AI continues this tradition, progressing through a gradual process of experimentation, adjustment, and stabilization.

Periods of technological transition inevitably challenge humans and institutions. Capabilities often emerge before they are fully understood or ready for implementation, causing anxiety, misclassification, misstatements of purpose, and sometimes fear. Public debate tends to oscillate between hype and hysteria, framing AI as either an unstoppable force or an existential threat. However, these reactions are typical during technological shifts, not indicators of destiny. AI is a powerful tool, but it is not the final stage of human progress. The lack of ongoing dialogue among

DOI: 10.1201/9781003744061-7

developers, users, policymakers, and other stakeholders has sharpened these polarized views and slowed institutional adaptation.

As the tension builds, the potential of next-generation networks becomes clearer. Progress in agentic AI, paired with tailored, carefully curated data and algorithms for specific tasks, signals a move away from fragile, poorly matched general-purpose systems toward more controlled, manageable, and goal-oriented structures. This shift requires improving how AI is categorized, integrated, and used within organizations so that its capabilities align with specific purposes rather than being broadly applied.

Next-generation networks do not fully remove AI's limitations nor replace human judgment. Instead, they restructure the deployment of intellectual capital by narrowing the focus, clarifying objectives, making reasoning more transparent, and embedding accountability in processes. Additionally, other forms of capital, including the physical infrastructure needed for agentic systems, are advancing in parallel, enabling more suitable, sustainable, and efficient deployment with reduced environmental footprints.

A familiar pattern is reemerging. Technologies typically progress from initial introduction through periods of uncertainty, and then through phases of fear and confusion, leading to detailed analysis and refinement, and eventually toward increased capital investment. AI is now moving into this next phase. Both institutions and individuals are shifting from disillusionment to a more disciplined evaluation of how AI can enhance their future potential. Viewing AI as part of a broader capital framework focused on intellectual capital enhances its relevance, purpose, and governance. While this process remains uneven and ongoing, it is now characterized less by speculation and more by potential and promise.

SIDEBAR 7.1   MISALIGNMENT TO MATURITY: ADVANCING HUMAN FLOURISHING THROUGH CAPITAL GROWTH

Problem: Early Phase AI Misalignment and Misclassification

- AI capability has expanded faster than the human, structural, and ethical capital required to govern it responsibly.
- General-purpose systems emphasize scale and speed at the expense of clarity, purpose, and accountability.

- Opacity, hallucinations, inherited bias, environmental strain, and social stress undermine trust, impair judgment, and weaken institutional resilience.
- These issues stem from a mismatch between capability and governance over time, rather than a technological breakdown.

Fix: Next-Generation Nets and Purpose-Trained Agentic AI

- Agentic AI systems are created for particular tasks, operate within defined boundaries, and have clear handoff points.
- Customized data and algorithmic training ensure that the system's behavior is aligned with its intended purpose, reducing the risk of generating generic or misleading outputs.
- Next-generation networks incorporate AI into managed workflows, enhancing transparency, traceability, and auditability of reasoning.
- Accountability is ensured through human oversight, defined escalation processes, and explicit institutional responsibilities.
- Improvements in effectiveness derive from discipline and specialization, not uncontrolled growth.
- Classification and deployment maturity enhance and strengthen capital, AI, and human resource development, guided by solid structural and ethical foundations.

Resolution: Human Flourishing and Measurable Capital Growth

- Human capital is cultivated to manage and utilize advanced types of intellectual capital.
- Intellectual capital is becoming more dependable, easier to interpret, better integrated, more customizable, and aligned with the mission.
- Structural capital reinforces decision-making processes, enhances transparency, streamlines workflows, and improves accountability.
- Ethical capital is realized through design limitations, governance, and responsible stewardship.
- Physical capital is maintained through cutting-edge applications, modularized technologies, and minimized environmental impact.

- Financial capital enhances long-term sustainability by bolstering trust, integrity, legitimacy, and resilience.
- Dignities are elevated, and the future of human flourishing is unveiled.

THE CHALLENGE: AI CREATES ECONOMIC, SOCIAL, AND HUMAN STRESS

Before exploring AI's potential, it is crucial to identify the current obstacles clearly. Recognizing unresolved issues is not pessimistic but a responsible step toward realignment. These problems do not stem from a lack of intelligence or creativity among engineers, programmers, or leaders, but rather from the societal, economic, physical, human, and institutional contexts in which AI operates. No technological deployment can fully predict all future challenges. Similar to human growth, introducing new technology involves an ongoing cycle of deployment, learning, adjustments, and redeployment.

Generative AI systems do not actually reason toward truth; instead, they detect and extend statistical patterns. While their outputs can seem coherent and convincing, their reliability remains uncertain. Sometimes, the results are insightful; other times, they are confidently false (Felin and Holweg 2024). The notion that AI can replace human reasoning stems from a mistaken view of the human mind as merely a simple input–output system. In reality, human reasoning is perceptual, deliberative, creative, and interpretive, functioning within moral, social, and contextual frameworks that cannot be reduced to mere pattern extension.

AI is trained on historical data and extrapolates probabilistically from this limited knowledge. This strength is evident in tasks that require consistency, replication, and classification, such as diagnostics or large-scale pattern recognition. However, it falls short and can even be harmful when used as a substitute for judgment, theory development, or responsibility. This limitation is not only technical but also stems from the gap between generating plausible outputs and creating knowledge that can be examined, justified, and trusted by human and institutional standards. When AI outputs cannot be questioned, understood, or explained, trust and accountability diminish. Moreover, AI systems trained on diverse data without proper refinement and broad algorithms may produce false results or hallucinations, and sometimes produce partially accurate, false information.

Bias is not just an occasional flaw but a deep-seated inheritance ingrained in data, model design, and the social histories behind training materials. AI systems trained on speech, market, media, policing, employment, and institutional records inevitably reflect past exclusions and inequalities, often even amplifying them at scale (Benjamin 2019). Additionally, new biases can arise through data selection, optimization goals, and feedback loops that favor efficiency over fairness. These issues are structural in nature rather than accidental. Historical social factors often influence output predictions, sometimes without a clear indication of how they influence results.

AI systems are increasingly integrated into complex socio-technical settings, influencing gaming platforms, autonomous vehicles, aircraft, military systems, logistics, and everyday automated tasks like sorting, tagging, and routing. Their performance depends not only on algorithms but also on imperfect sensors, limited training data, and unpredictable physical factors. No dataset or algorithm can account for the full spectrum of real-world variability. Systems using lidar, radar, cameras, global positioning satellite, and wireless telemetry operate faster and more efficiently, but also become new targets for vulnerabilities. Under unfamiliar or rapidly evolving conditions, their performance can decline unpredictably or without clear explanation (Miller et al. 2024; Tsvetanov 2025).

As deployment scales up, initial excitement often gives way to reevaluation. The accumulation of models, tools, integrations, and platforms makes decision pathways harder to trace. Limited interpretability of data and algorithms leads to contested outcomes, undermining trust in AI-supported decisions across sectors such as business, government, education, and civil society (Burrell 2016).

AI is not purely digital; it relies on physical resources such as capital, energy, materials, and land. Semiconductor manufacturing depends on delicate mineral supply chains, specialized chemicals, and vast amounts of water to produce ultrapure water used in manufacturing. Data centers consume significant electricity and require extensive cooling, often located in communities affected by data center-generated heat, noise, zoning issues, and environmental concerns. Training large AI models uses energy comparable to that of entire vehicle fleets (Strubell, Ganesh, and McCallum 2019).

Roy Schwartz et al. (2020) draw an important distinction between resource-intensive methods focused on accuracy and sustainable AI approaches that emphasize efficiency and environmental friendliness.

These choices shape AI's environmental footprint and future sustainability. Schwartz's insights point to a more focused AI approach.

Strategic pressures exacerbate these challenges. The limited availability of advanced chips and essential minerals has heightened geopolitical rivalries over supply chains and industrial infrastructure. At the same time, AI is increasingly embedded in military platforms, surveillance networks, and autonomous decision-making systems that operate faster than traditional processes and, in many cases, outpace human judgment. Paul Scharre (2018) cautions that AI-enabled systems may act so swiftly that they cannot be easily questioned, halted, or reversed after deployment, raising significant concerns about escalation, accountability, and conflict management.

Financial structures are showing signs of stress. Creating and running large-scale AI infrastructure demands huge capital investments in land, power, cooling, chips, and specialized labor. When these expenses surpass a company's internal cash flows, firms tend to turn to corporate bonds, private credit, and structured financing methods (Raitano 2025; Morgan Stanley Research 2025). Off-balance-sheet arrangements can maintain favorable credit ratings while hiding actual exposure and shifting risks elsewhere. Experts warn that capital requirements might grow faster than sustainable revenues, echoing past cycles where financial optimism surpassed economic fundamentals (Storm 2025; Noffsinger et al. 2025).

Employment effects offer a clear view of the human impact of these pressures. Generative AI is now widely used by information workers across sectors, reshaping how jobs are structured, how tasks are assigned, and early career opportunities. Although overall employment may still increase, opportunities shift unevenly by age and experience. Workers in early career roles, most vulnerable to AI, face significant disruption. Entry-level positions decline, paths to professional judgment narrow, and shifts in employment patterns are more visible than wage changes. When AI is used to support human work through careful governance, these impacts can be reduced. Without governance, capital substitution pressures dominate (Brynjolfsson, Chandar, and Chen 2025).

The core issue extends beyond merely counting jobs. Entry-level positions are crucial environments where judgment, responsibility, and professional identity are cultivated. When automation reduces or eliminates these roles, the development of human capital diminishes. While short-term productivity gains are tempting, they can mask the gradual erosion of human capital that will be essential for society, organizations, and families in the future.

Finally, large-scale automation can create systemic vulnerabilities. As AI integrates into sectors such as transportation, energy, finance, logistics, emergency response, and communication, failures can spread, with a single point of failure affecting entire communities, organizations, and societies. The danger doesn't stem from malicious intent but from over-confidence. As systems seem more capable, human oversight often diminishes. Hans Jonas (1985) warned that technological power without adequate ethical responsibility can lead to such risks. Therefore, the challenges facing AI are not solely technical; they are also human, institutional, economic, and ecological.

The pressures related to AI do not happen in isolation. They occur where the fast-growing intellectual capital interacts with human, structural, financial, physical, and ethical capital, which tend to evolve more slowly and unevenly. Table 7.1 outlines how current AI deployment strains each type of capital. This is not a list of failures but a diagnostic tool for early misalignments during integration. These pressure points help

TABLE 7.1　Current AI Pressures on the Six Forms of Capital

Form of Capital	Capital Strain Introduced by AI	Representative Themes
Human Capital	Displacement risk, skill erosion, contraction of entry-level roles, over-reliance on automation, and reduced opportunities for formation.	Substitution of routine cognitive tasks, weakened early career pathways, labor adjustment visible more in employment than wages, temptation to replace judgment rather than develop it (Brynjolfsson et al. 2025; Jonas 1985).
Intellectual Capital	Unreliable outputs, hallucinations, limited explainability, inherited bias, imitation without understanding, difficulty reconstructing reasoning.	Systems predict patterns rather than truth; historical inequities are reproduced; layered tools obscure causal attribution; trust erodes when knowledge claims cannot be examined or justified (Felin and Holweg 2024; Benjamin 2019; Burrell 2016).
Structural Capital	Governance gaps, accountability diffusion, rapid deployment ahead of oversight, geopolitical escalation, fragile interdependencies.	Organizational and social governance gaps. Military and surveillance integration outpaces policy; public and institutional accountability lags; oversight weakens as systems scale across sectors and borders (Scharre 2018).

(*Continued*)

TABLE 7.1   (Continued)

Form of Capital	Capital Strain Introduced by AI	Representative Themes
Financial Capital	High capital intensity, structural borrowing, cash burn, opaque financing, valuation risk, systemic exposure.	AI infrastructure financed through bonds, private credit, and special-purpose vehicles; borrowing becomes a structural financial system weakness; expectations may exceed long-term earnings capacity (Raitano 2025; Morgan Stanley Research 2025).
Physical Capital	Resource extraction pressures, water and energy demand, land conflict, environmental degradation, infrastructure vulnerability.	Semiconductor and data-center expansion consume minerals, water, land, and power; localized heat, noise, grid stress, and emissions provoke community resistance (Strubell et al. 2019; Schwartz et al. 2020).
Ethical Capital	Erosion of trust, normalization of bias, decision speed exceeding moral deliberation, abdication of responsibility, unequal impact.	Systems operate faster than ethical governance; harms concentrate among vulnerable populations; non-transparency undermines consent and fairness; competition displaces restraint (Benjamin 2019; Scharre 2018).

explain why AI challenges go beyond performance or accuracy, involving the management of capital frameworks that ultimately influence whether technological progress advances human well-being.

These pressures do not determine the ultimate shape of AI, nor do they dismiss its potential. Instead, they highlight a common pattern in early technological adoption: capabilities outpace governance, investment alignment, and organizational growth. As AI advances, gains in efficiency, dependability, environmental impact, and integration are already evident. The future of AI depends on how well knowledge is generated, effectiveness is measured, applications are managed, and whether governance can synchronize evolving intellectual and structural assets with ethical goals and human well-being.

THE PROMISE: NEXT-GENERATION AI, MEANING, MEASUREMENT, AND MANAGEMENT

Viewing capital as a framework naturally yields what can be called economic oncology: an organized perspective that distinguishes between growth that enhances human well-being and that which subtly undermines it. AI is not inherently beneficial simply because it can scale. As in biological systems, technological progress can be either beneficial or harmful. Beneficial growth reinforces capital assets and boosts human potential, while harmful growth drains value, disrupts development, and distorts the societal relationships essential for stability.

The responsible future of AI should be grounded in meaningful and aligned objectives, focused on positively impacting humans and fostering human well-being and social progress.

SIDEBAR 7.2   THE PROMISE OF CAPITAL-AWARE AI GOVERNANCE

The potential of next-generation AI is not just about speed, scale, or independence. Instead, it depends on whether advancing technology enhances the fundamental structures that support human well-being. Effective AI governance that respects capital relies on three enduring principles.

Meaning: AI must be grounded in a clear understanding of its purpose. Classification helps determine whether a system promotes human development, organizational accountability, and ethical goals, or replaces them. Technology only has significance when its position within the capital framework is clearly defined.

Measurement: AI assessment should go beyond technical and financial outcomes. It involves analyzing and measuring how AI systems affect human, intellectual, structural, financial, physical, and ethical resources over time. Assessing AI's impact on dignity is an outcome assessment. The focus is on what AI produces and what it enhances or diminishes.

Management: AI should be deliberately directed to support human knowledge creation and well-being rather than to replace judgment. This ensures that automation supports human learning, preserves accountability, and enhances the relational environments where knowledge, trust, and responsibility are built. Ultimately, meaning, measurement, and management guide AI to its appropriate purpose: fostering sustainable capacity, legitimate institutions, and long-term human well-being.

A disciplined approach to assessing, managing, and organizing AI closely aligns with Ikujiro Nonaka's (1994) theory of knowledge. Nonaka asserts that knowledge extends beyond stored information; it is an active human process rooted in context, belief, and purpose, developed through interaction and validated by practice. Knowledge becomes meaningful only when it is embedded, interpreted, shared, and embodied through action. From this perspective, AI systems alone do not constitute knowledge; they become part of organizational knowledge only when they participate in the human processes that create and validate meaning.

Knowledge creation unfolds through an uneven, spiral movement between tacit and explicit knowledge. As Ikujiro Nonaka and Hirotaka Takeuchi (1995) explain, this knowledge spiral is driven by socialization, externalization, combination, and internalization. It underpins both human and organizational learning and innovation. AI supports this process by assisting with documentation, synthesis, pattern recognition, and retrieval, but it leaves interpretation, judgment, and learning to humans, where the full potential of the knowledge spiral can be realized. This spiral illustrates the interaction between human and intellectual capital.

AI can play a role in this process by enhancing the environment for transformation and leveraging its advanced capabilities to effectively support knowledge development, learning progress, character growth, and improved judgment. This next-generation human–AI relationship shifts from being merely transactional to truly transformational.

Ikujiro Nonaka and Noboru Konno (1998) characterize the transformative environments that support this process as *Ba*, shared contexts where dialogue, reflection, and relationships turn information into knowledge. In this framework, knowledge is seen as relational rather than transactional. Within these environments, technology serves as an intellectual partner rather than as an authority. AI does not generate meaning on its own, but it can offer structure, insights, and curated perspectives that support human understanding and informed action in a relational way.

From a capital development perspective, economic oncology serves as the managerial counterpart to this knowledge framework. Positioning AI within the capital structure assigns social, organizational, and individual significance. Assessing its effects on capital reveals how it influences human well-being. Intentional management of AI ensures these technologies develop in ways that support human and other forms of capital. Capital-conscious AI governance goes beyond mere technical supervision; it embodies a form of knowledge leadership that fosters both immediate and long-term capital growth by enhancing human skills and guiding capital toward meaningful, sustainable progress within organizations and society.

This reframing shifts leadership focus from optimization to stewardship. Leaders, regulators, engineers, technologists, educators, economists, and civic authorities need to recognize where AI enhances capacity, displaces traditional structures, offers economic benefits, and subtly undermines the social foundations of trust and cooperation. Future AI assessments will go beyond technical performance or financial gains and instead be evaluated by their contribution to societal capital (Jonas 1985).

DISRUPTION TO DESIGN: NEXT-GENERATION AI AND THE REORDERING OF CAPITAL

Within an economic oncology framework, every AI deployment is a hypothesis about its impact on capital. It requires evaluation before, during, and after deployment to assess whether it enhances or undermines the foundations of human well-being. The key concern is how AI influences the distribution and allocation of capital, which in turn shapes social and organizational dignity and well-being.

Early AI deployments challenged all six forms of capital because capabilities outpaced design discipline. However, the emerging trend is different. Next-generation AI increasingly comprises agentic, distributed systems that operate within defined boundaries, collaborate with humans, and conserve resources rather than waste them. These bounded, agentic systems enable modularity, curation, and customization of data, algorithms, and training methods. This transition shifts from a broad, one-size-fits-all strategy to a tailored, purpose-driven approach.

Agentic AI systems consist of bounded agents that aim to achieve specific goals within defined boundaries. These agents can sequence multiple tasks, evaluate intermediate results, request clarification, and return work to human decision-makers at designated points. Rather than generating answers in a single, opaque step, they organize work into stages such as gathering information, testing assumptions, verifying outcomes, documenting decisions, and escalating uncertainty. This approach divides complex tasks into smaller, iterative steps, enabling agentic systems to go beyond simple prompt–response interactions while maintaining human oversight and accountability (Wooldridge 2009; Park et al. 2023).

This structured approach directs AI-supported work through clear rules, workflows, and oversight mechanisms that reflect structural and ethical considerations. As a result, processes become more transparent and traceable, enabling outputs to be reviewed, questioned, and improved over time. When paired with disciplined scope and task-specific design, these phased workflows can minimize unnecessary computation and reduce the energy and resource costs associated with indiscriminate scaling (Strubell, Ganesh, and McCallum 2019; Schwartz et al. 2020).

At the same time, next-generation AI is becoming more decentralized. Computation is performed closer to data sources, enabling decisions within departments, facilities, hospitals, classrooms, geographic locations, warehouses, and communities. This shift away from large centralized systems reduces energy and natural resource use, mitigates systemic risks, and reintroduces human oversight at practical levels. These technological advancements change how AI engages with all forms of capital.

Human Capital: Formation Preserved or Displaced

Next-generation AI serves as a scaffolding system rather than replacing human development. Agentic tools offer options, test ideas, and encourage reflection, with human review at key points in the process. Junior professionals still perform the work, supported by structured processes that accelerate learning without sacrificing vital experience. While productivity rises, responsibility and judgment remain with humans. Organizations may need fewer junior staff, but those trained within these systems develop stronger human capital and ethical skills, preparing them for future leadership rather than restricting their professional growth. The governing condition is clear. Decision rights and accountability remain with humans.

Intellectual Capital: Knowledge Strengthened or Simulated

Early deployment AI predicts patterns without reasoning to understand them; it relies on knowledge. Agentic AI changes this by making reasoning explicit rather than hidden. It involves breaking tasks down, documenting sources, scrutinizing assumptions, and revealing uncertainty rather than hiding it. This approach exposes complexity, allowing humans to interpret, challenge, and enhance conclusions. Information becomes examinable, testable, and improvable rather than passively accepted. Thus, transparency enhances the significance, measurement, and management of knowledge, enabling next-generation intellectual capital to actively engage in the knowledge cycle rather than merely generate outputs (Phillips et al. 2021).

For next-generation AI to become a trusted partner in advancing knowledge, transparency is essential. This means making AI reasoning and sources clear, explicitly showing uncertainty, handling complexity through structured steps, and promoting learning instead of just generating seemingly plausible but potentially incorrect results.

Structural Capital: Governance Reinforced or Bypassed

Next-generation AI overcomes traditional limitations by integrating customizable governance into workflows. Training on specific datasets provides additional control, allowing organizations to restrict inputs and influence results more intentionally. Agentic systems ensure approval processes, maintain audit logs, document decision paths, and flag anomalies for human review. Distributed architectures support these controls locally, making them accessible for inspection, challenge, and correction, rather than confining them to distant, less controllable systems (Balasubramaniam et al. 2023).

The main condition is structural subordination. As next-generation AI evolves to become more adaptable, able to handle complexity and changing circumstances, and responsive to context-specific limits, it can enhance and support structural capital instead of circumventing it. As AI advances, it can also simulate how structural rules influence interactions across various types of capital and affect mission or market results, all while remaining subordinate to human oversight.

Financial Capital: Sustainable Value or Accumulated Risk

Large centralized AI systems often demand significant capital investment, usually financed via debt and complex structures that hide exposure. While growth may seem impressive, hidden risks are building up within organizational and financial systems.

Next-generation AI minimizes this risk by focusing on efficiency and distribution. Smaller, task-focused models, localized processing, and phased deployment help lower peak infrastructure needs, ensure steadier cash flow, and decrease the risk of single-point failures. As a result, capital investment becomes incremental and accountable rather than speculative.

The core principle is prudence. Financial discipline goes beyond technical aspects; it is fundamentally ethical. When AI investments match genuine capacity and focus on long-term value, innovation stays sustainable instead of being exploitative, and risks are minimized instead of shifted.

Physical Capital: Stewardship Practiced or Resources Extracted

Large-scale models require significant resources such as energy, water, land, and minerals, which can place substantial burdens on communities and ecosystems. Achieving small improvements in accuracy often involves high physical costs.

Next-generation AI takes a different path. Distributed and edge processing, or processing near the source of data generation, reduces data transfer and cooling requirements. Smaller models require fewer chips and consume less power. Federated learning reduces the need for centralized storage. AI systems are increasingly self-optimizing their energy, cooling cycles, and water use. When combined with renewable resources, lifecycle hardware considerations, and responsible settings, the physical footprint decreases even as capabilities expand.

Visibility is the key condition. When physical costs are evaluated over the entire lifecycle instead of being hidden in abstractions, design decisions are affected. Stewardship then becomes a sign of technological maturity.

Ethical Capital: Trust Built or Quietly Eroded

Ethical erosion tends to develop gradually rather than suddenly. It occurs as organizations or societies move from explaining decisions to automating processes, and from making judgments to relying on system outputs.

Next-generation AI enhances ethical standards by pausing decision-making when dignity calls for human involvement. Agentic workflows ensure human approval at key points, keeping responsibility transparent and accountable. Distributed systems limit the impact of errors, making it easier to identify, correct, and learn from mistakes. As AI advances, it can embed organizational structures and ethical guidelines into its analysis, enabling systems to predict how decisions influence trust, responsibility, and social dynamics rather than just optimizing for outcomes. Consequently, explanations, appeals, and corrections become standard parts of the process, not just rare responses (Balasubramaniam et al. 2023).

The key principle is restraint. Trust increases when organizations show that efficiency does not take precedence over conscience. Ethical capital is strengthened when technology stays within limits, remains contestable, and is held accountable.

TABLE 7.2   Capital-Aware AI: Conditions of Healthy Growth Across the Six Forms
of Capital

Form of Capital	How Next-Generation AI Strengthens Capital	Representative Signals of Health
Human	Preserves formation and judgment	Apprenticeships protected, decision rights remain human
Intellectual	Clarifies knowledge creation	Transparent reasoning, documented uncertainty
Structural	Reinforces governance	Auditable workflows, human-in-the-loop oversight
Financial	Supports sustainable value	Lifecycle costing, staged investment
Physical	Reduces resource burden	Distributed processing, lower water, environmental impact, and energy intensity
Ethical	Builds trust and legitimacy	Explainability, consent, restraint

Table 7.2 summarizes the conditions that enable next-generation AI to
promote healthy growth, illustrating how careful design and implementation
can reinforce, rather than weaken, the foundations of human well-being.

AI AS A PURPOSEFUL INTELLECTUAL CAPITAL COMPANION

AI functions as a form of organizational or societal capital. Each implementation alters the makeup, vitality, and path of human, intellectual,
structural, financial, physical, and ethical assets. The main mistake of
early AI development was not ambition but misclassification. Viewing AI
as human capital overlooks judgment and decision-making. Seeing it as
structural capital diminishes agency and accountability. Imagining AI as
autonomous leads to the silent abdication of ethical responsibility.

Proper classification restores coherence. When AI aligns with human,
organizational, and societal goals through meaning, measurement, and
management, it creates capital. This capital forms the foundation of dignity and human flourishing.

This emphasis on human flourishing explains why capital is the right
lens for diagnosis. Capital is the human leverage for progress and dignity.
Technology and economic activity aim not merely to accelerate processes
but to enhance human action and societal well-being. When properly
directed, AI serves as a disciplined tool in this endeavor.

AI continues a long tradition of expanding human capabilities through intellectual pursuit. Historically, innovations like literacy, law, accounting, engineering, and digital infrastructure initially caused disruption but eventually led to transformation. Over time, they revealed deeper insights into what societies could create and what they valued. Today, AI is part of this ongoing legacy, contributing to human flourishing.

TAKEAWAYS

- Technological progress is not a goal. AI is important because it transforms the environments in which humans learn, govern, work, and thrive.

- Legacy AI deployments revealed a gap between technical ability and institutional readiness. These pressures indicate an early phase of integration rather than the technology's ultimate form.

- Agentic and distributed AI systems alter how value is generated by making processes transparent, maintaining human oversight, and reducing dependence on centralized infrastructure.

- Intellectual capital increases when AI helps clarify knowledge creation, reveals uncertainty, and facilitates learning instead of just mimicking understanding.

- Structural capital is strengthened when AI is developed to support governance, accountability, and institutional memory instead of bypassing these functions.

- Financial capital remains secure when AI investments adhere to disciplined capital budgeting, lifecycle costing, and transparent risk management procedures.

- Physical capital remains intact when AI design emphasizes efficiency, distributed processing, and the responsible use of energy, water, and land resources.

- Ethical capital is strengthened when AI stays within the limits of human responsibility, explainability, consent, restraint, and agency.

- Healthy growth depends on disciplined design. AI enhances human well-being when it is directed by clear meaning, effective measurement, and careful management.

WORKS CITED

Ansley, Chris, and Enda Curran. 2025, December 18. "How AI Borrowing Could Emerge as a Problem for the Fed." *Bloomberg*. Accessed January 5, 2026. https://www.bloomberg.com/news/newsletters/2025-12-18/how-ai-borrowing-could-emerge-as-a-problem-for-the-federal-reserve?embedded-checkout=true

Arendt, Hannah. 1998. *The Human Condition* (2nd ed.). Chicago: The University of Chicago Press.

Balasubramaniam, Nagadivya, Marjo Kauppinen, Antti Rannisto, Kari Hiekkanen, and Sari Kujala. 2023. "Transparency and Explainability of AI Systems: From Ethical Guidelines to Requirements." *Information and Software Technology* 159, 1–15. doi: 10.1016/j.infsof.2023.107197

Benjamin, Ruha. 2019. *Race After Technology: Abolitionist Tools for the New Jim Code*. Medford, MA: Polity Press.

Brynjolfsson, Erik, Bharat Chandar, and Ruyu Chen. 2025, August 26. "Canaries in the Coal Mine? Six Facts about the Recent Employment Effects of Artificial Intelligence." *Stanford Digital Economy Lab*. Accessed January 5, 2026. https://digitaleconomy.stanford.edu/wp-content/uploads/2025/08/Canaries_BrynjolfssonChandarChen.pdf

Burrell, Jenna. 2016. "How the Machine 'Thinks:' Understanding Opacity in Machine Learning Algorithms." *Big Data & Society* 3 (1). Accessed January 5, 2026. https://papers.ssrn.com/sol3/papers.cfm?abstract_id=2660674

Deloitte. n.d. "Agentic Enterprise 2028." *Deloitte*. Accessed January 5, 2026. https://www.deloitte.com/us/en/what-we-do/capabilities/applied-artificial-intelligence/articles/agentic-ai-enterprise-2028.html?id=us:2ps:3gl:aisgm26:awa:CONS:nonem:K0218784:111725:kwd-2448184523662:188372336109:784136672833::Brand_AI-SGO_BU_K0218784_Goog

Felin, Teppo, and Matthias Holweg. 2024. "Theory Is All You Need: AI, Human Cognition, and Causal Reasoning." *Strategy Science* 9 (4): 346–371.

Jonas, Hans. 1985. *The Imperative of Responsibility: In Search of an Ethics for the Technological Age*. Chicago: University of Chicago Press.

Kinder, Tabby. 2025, December 24. "Tech Groups Shift US$120 billion of AI Data Centre Debt Off Balance Sheets." *Financial Times*. Accessed January 5, 2026. https://financialpost.com/financial-times/tech-groups-ai-data-centre-debt-balance-sheets

Miller, Tymoteusz, Irmina Durlik, Ewelina Kostecka, Piotr Borkowski, and Adrianna Lobodzinkska. 2024, September. "A Critical AI View on Autonomous Vehicle Navigation: The Growing Danger." *Electronics* 13 (18): 26 pp. doi: 10.3390/electronics13183660

Morahan, Chris, Dana Cease, and Stuart Muter. 2025, December 1. "AI Funding: The Bull and Bear Investment Cases." *Morgan Stanley Insights*. Accessed January 5, 2026. https://www.morganstanley.com/im/en-us/institutional-investor/insights/articles/bull-and-bear-investment-cases.html

Morgan Stanley Research. 2025, July 16. "Bridging a $1.5tr Data Center Financing Gap." *Morgan Stanley Research*. Accessed January 5, 2026. https://www.scribd.com/document/903369274/Bridging-a-1-5tr-Data-Center

Noffsinger, Jesse, Mark Patel, Pankaj Sachdeva, Arjita Bhan, Haley Chang, and Maria Goodpaster. 2025, April 28. "The Cost of Compute: A $7 Trillion Race to Scale Data Centers." *McKinsey & Company Technology, Media & Telecommunications*. Accessed January 5, 2026. https://www.mckinsey.com/industries/technology-media-and-telecommunications/our-insights/the-cost-of-compute-a-7-trillion-dollar-race-to-scale-data-centers

Nonaka, Ikujiro. 1994. "A Dynamic Theory of Organizational Knowledge Creation." *Organization Science* 5 (1): 14–37.

Nonaka, Ikujiro, and Noboru Konno. 1998. "The Concept of "Ba": Building a Foundation for Knowledge Creation." *California Management Review* 40 (3): 40–54.

Nonaka, Ikujiro, and Hirotaka Takeuchi. 1995. *The Knowledge-Creating Company: How Japanese Companies Create the Dynamics of Innovation*. New York: Oxford University Press.

Park, Joon Sung, Joseph C. O'Brien, Carrie J. Cai, Meredith Ringel Morris, Percy Liang, and Michael S. Bernstein. 2023, August 6. "Generative Agents: Interactive Simulacra of Human Behavior." *ArXiv*. Accessed January 5, 2026. https://arxiv.org/abs/2304.03442

Phillips, P. Jonathon, Carina A. Hahn, Peter C. Fontana, Amy N. Yates, Kristen Greene, David A. Broniatowski, and Mark A. Przybocki. 2021. *Four Principles of Explainable Artificial Intelligence*. NISTIR 8312. Gaithersburg, MD: National Institute of Standards and Technology (NIST). https://tsapps.nist.gov/publication/get_pdf.cfm?pub_id=933399

Raitano, Lucy. 2025, December 12. "Five Debt Hotspots in the AI Data Centre Boom." *Reuters*. Accessed January 5, 2026. https://www.reuters.com/business/finance/five-debt-hotspots-ai-data-centre-boom-2025-12-11

Russell, Stuart. 2019. *Human Compatible: Artificial Intelligence and the Problem of Control*. New York: Viking.

Scharre, Paul. 2018. *Army of None: Autonomous Weapons and the Future of War*. New York: W.W. Norton & Company.

Schwartz, Roy, Jesse Dodge, Noah A. Smith, and Oren Etzioni. 2020. "Green AI." *Communications of the ACM* (ACM) 63 (12): 54–63.

Stewart, Thomas A. 1997. *Intellectual Capital: The New Wealth of Organizations*. New York: Currency.

Storm, Servaas. 2025, December. "The U.S. Is Betting the Economy on "Scaling" AI: Where Is the Intelligence When One Needs It?" *Institute for New Economic Thinking*. Accessed January 5, 2026. https://www.ineteconomics.org/research/research-papers/the-u-s-is-betting-the-economy-on-scaling-ai-where-is-the-intelligence-when-one-needs-it

Strubell, Emma, Ananya Ganesh, and Andrew McCallum. 2019. "Energy and Policy Considerations for Deep Learning in NLP." In *Proceedings of the 57th Annual Meeting of the Association for Computational Linguistics*, edited by Anna Korhonen, David Traum and Lluis Marquez, 3645–3650. Florence, Italy: Association for Computational Linguistics.

Tsvetanov, Filip. 2025. "Hardware Challenges in AI Sensors and Innovative Approaches to Overcome Them." *Alexandroupolis Greece: Proceedings of International Conference on Electronics, Engineering Physics and Earth Science (EEPES 2025)*, 19.

Wooldridge, Michael. 2009. *An Introduction to MultiAgent Systems* (2nd ed.). Hoboken, NJ: Wiley.

Yao, Shunyu, Jeffrey Zhao, Dian Yu, Nan Du, Izhak Shafran, Karthik Narasimhan, and Yuan Cao. 2023, March 10. "ReAct: Synergizing Reasoning and Acting in Language Models." *ArXiv*. Accessed January 5, 2026. https://arxiv.org/abs/2210.03629

Index

Pages in *italics* refer to figures, pages in **bold**-*italics* refer to boxes and pages in **bold** refer to tables. Pages followed by "n" refer to notes.

Roos, J., 4, 7, 10
Rosenberg, N., 12
routines, organizational, 7, 9–11, 13, **19**, 75, 96, **109**, *121*
Russell, S., 96
Ryan, R. M., 65

S

Sahni, N. R., 31
Samraik, M., **111**
Sawyer, R. K., 105, 124
Scharre, P., 144, **145–146**
Schivelbusch, W., 20
Schultz, T. W., 5, **6**, *39*
Schumpeter, J. A., 14, 21, 30, 106
Schwartz, R., 143–144, **146**, 150
secondary education, 122–126
Sen, A., 17, *18*
Serafeim, G., *39*, 42, 73, 107
Shiva, V., 20
Shonkoff, J. P., 54
Sisodia, R., 74
Skitka, L. J., 78
Smith, A., 27–28
social learning, 51, 53, 59–61
Solow, R. M., 12, 29, 38
stakeholder capital, 41–42
stakeholders, 17, *18*, 22, 42, 45–46, 70, 75, 77, 80–81, 99–102, 107, *129*, 140
stakeholder trust, 17, *18*, *39*, 42, *116*
Stanford Institute for Human-Centered Artificial Intelligence (HAI), 79
Steinberg, L., 122
Sternberg, R. J., 105
Stewart, T. A., 4, 7–9, 13, 28, *39*, 96
Stiglitz, J., *16*
Storm, S., 144
Strubell, E., 143, **146**, 150
structural capital, 7, 9–10, *11*, 16–17, **19**, 36–41, 45, 75, 77, 81–83, *84*, 95–96, 101, **111**, *121*, *126*, *129*, *132*, 134, *141*, 145, 151, 153–154
Sugrue, T. J., 21
Sunstein, C. R., 60

sustainability, *13*, 14, 17–18, *19*, 42, 74–75, 101, 107, *142*
sustainability practices, 42, 107
systems thinking, 10, *18–19*, 20–22
Syverson, C., 12

T

tacit knowledge, 36, **109**
Takeuchi, H., 148
Taylor, C., 3, 10, *11*
technology, 1–3, *9*, 20–21, 22n1, 27–31, 40–41, 47n1, 53, *57*, 95–97, 102, 108, 112n2, 116, 120, 131, *147*, 153
Teece, D., 12
Tennessee Valley Authority, 21
tertiary education, 124–130
Throsby, D., 96
Tidd, J., 106
Tillich, P., 58
Topol, E., 31, 47n2, 103, 108, **111**
trust, 10, *11*, 14, 17–18, 21, 38, 44, 58–59, 79–82, *84*, 90, 101–105, **110**, 130–135
Tsvetanov, F., 143
Tufekci, Z., 103
Turing, A., *97*
Turing Test, 97
Twenge, J. M., 120

U

UK Parliament, 74
Unilever Corporation, 87–88
United Nations, 74, 107
United States Congress, 74
universities, 126–129
US Copyright Office, **110**

V

value creation, 4–5, *16*, 20, 30, 38, 41–42, *43*, 62, 73, 77, 80, 82, 85–86, 90–91, 98–99, 101–104, 107
VanLehn, K., *57*

For Product Safety Concerns and Information please contact our EU
representative GPSR@taylorandfrancis.com
Taylor & Francis Verlag GmbH, Kaufingerstraße 24, 80331 München, Germany

www.ingramcontent.com/pod-product-compliance
Lightning Source LLC
Chambersburg PA
CBHW070941250726
48663CB00001B/19